Brassey's **BOOK OF UNIFORMS**

TIM NEWARK

BOOK OF UNIFORMS

To Victoria, a real gem

The author would like to thank the following for their help with the book:
Louis Chalmers of The Plumery, Dawn Wood and Andrew Clark ,
Mike Buteux of Hobson's and Sons, Malcolm Fisher of Regimentals,
Trooper Mackenzie and Trooper Crawford of the Life Guards, John Watt
of Strines Textiles, Gerald Moulin of Angels and Bermans, Ron Field,
Stephen Bull, Martin Brayley, James Scarlett, Bernard Sutherland, Robin
Smith, Neil Gibson, Michael Dyer Associates, Military Illustrated, National
Army Museum, British Library, and Lucy Wildman for a jolly day out.

Special thanks to Peter Newark and Quentin Newark.

All the illustrations reproduced in this book are from Peter Newark's
Military Pictures (3 Barton Buildings, off Queen Square, Bath BA1 2JR,
tel: 01225 334213), except for those appearing on: p.17 Richard
Hook/Military Illustrated; p.21 Military Illustrated; p.26 Dawn Wood; p.33
James Scarlett; p.38 Ron Poulter/Military Illustrated; p.55 Alan Thrower/Ron
Field; p.63 Bryan Fosten/Military Illustrated; p.67 Robin Smith; pp.80–81
Malcolm Fisher/Regimentals; p.82 Stephen Bull; p.84–85 Malcolm
Fisher/Regimentals; p.94 Martin Brayley; p.99 Malcolm Fisher/Regimentals;
p.103–104 Martin Brayley; p.107 Paul Miraldi; p.115 Stephen
Andrews/Military Illustrated; p.139 Carlton TV. Special photography by
Michael Dyer Associates Ltd. (tel: 0171 836 8354).

First English edition 1998

UK editorial offices:
Brassey's Ltd., 33 John Street, London WC1N 2AT
UK orders:
Marston Book Services, PO Box 269, Abingdon OX14 4SD
North American Orders:
Brassey's Inc., PO Box 960, Herndon, VA20172, USA

Tim Newark has asserted his moral right to be identified as the author
of this work

Library of Congress Cataloging in Publication Data available
British Library Cataloguing in Publication Data
A catalogue record for this book is available from the British Library

ISBN 1 85753 243 0

Designed by Atelier Works
Edited by Tim Newark for Brassey's
Printed and bound in Singapore under the supervision
of M.R.M. Graphics Ltd., Winslow, Buckinghamshire

CONTENTS

Uniforms of the Armies of the
Six Great Powers of Europe in
1904: Russia, Germany, Great
Britain, France, Italy and
Austria-Hungary. This painting
by H. A. Ogden represents the
colourful apogee of European
uniforms before the wars of the
20th century reduced everyone
to either khaki or grey.

A SOLDIER'S LIFE

The life of a soldier is a constant struggle between civilisation and barbarity. On the one hand, he is the upholder of national security and order, a beacon of righteousness; in battle, he must maintain discipline and self-control to survive the onslaught of the enemy. But on the other hand, away from the light of public scrutiny, he pursues the darker demands of his profession – death and destruction – he lays waste his enemy's land and instills the greatest fear in his enemy's people.

The history of the evolution of soldiers' uniforms is a history of these two opposites. The struggle between civilisation and barbarity is reflected in the very fabric, the very design, the very combination of soldiers' clothes. Their uniformity and smartness speaks of reassuring discipline and control, but the fur-lining, the bearskin cap, the camouflage smeared face, all evoke a more primitive world of hunting, disguise, and death. The uniformed soldier may be part of an army controlled by law and order, but as an individual he is a professional killer. This book tells the story of the secret meaning of uniforms.

Tim Newark, London, 1997

THE MEANING OF UNIFORMS

ORIGIN OF UNIFORMS

It is no surprise that military uniforms should first appear in Europe towards the end of the 17th century. For over a hundred years previously, the great states of Western Europe had been savaged by the worst kind of warfare. Civil war fuelled by religious and cultural hatred had reduced much of the continent to a battlefield. Nations were divided, communities dislocated, populations expelled, helpless people massacred, towns besieged and burnt, and everywhere warriors roamed the land in search of loot. The medieval sense of order and authority provided by the Catholic Church and the great supranational landowners had been challenged and in many places defeated.

In the Netherlands, from 1559 to 1648, Dutch Protestants fought for their independence from the Spanish Hapsburgs. In France, from 1562 to 1653, Protestants and rebels fought against the monarchy. In northern Europe, among the German states where the Reformation first took hold, antagonism between Catholics and Protestants exploded in the ferociously destructive Thirty Years War of 1618 to 1648. In England, the Catholic monarchy was overthrown in a series of wars and uprisings between 1642 and 1689.

These conflicts endured for decades and when combat lulled between campaigns and battles, armies lived off the land and the civilian population became used to a world in which soldiers acted as bandits to maintain their strength and their coffers in readiness for the next combat. Their world was militarised and law and order depended on the arbitrary rule of armed power. It is little wonder that as this terrible period of civil wars came to an end and national governments began to reassert themselves, there should be a great desire for order and one of the first demands was that military power should be subject to civilian control. Kings and governments should control armies, not the other way round. The era of independent warlords was over and one sign that this was so was the appearance of soldiers neatly clad in national uniforms.

In England, following the restoration of royal power in 1660, the degree of detail proscribed for the royal body-guard advanced quickly from simply a red tunic to something more elaborate. In 1685, at King James II's coronation, his First Foot Guards, the soldiers closest to him were clad in the following outfit: 'The Private Soldiers were all new Cloathed in coats of Red broad cloth, Lined

German *Landsknecht* mercenaries of the 16th century. Freelance warriors such as these terrified the civilian populations of Europe and were renowned for wearing a riot of colours and materials in their clothing. It was partly in reaction to the disorder symbolised by such soldiers that uniforms came into being.

and Faced with Blew; Their Hats were Black, Laced about with Silver, turned up and garnished with Blew Ribbands. Their Breeches were Blew Broad Cloth, and their Stockings of Blew Worsted.'[1] Since the Middle Ages, companies of soldiers had frequently worn the marks of their commanders, indicated by a coloured sash or plume, or coloured tunic bearing an heraldic device. Such devices were usually worn by the immediate bodyguard or house guard of a lord or monarch, establishing that the soldiers closest to him were in fact his servants. But the complexity of these late 17th century uniforms was something new and different, a more profound attempt at control.

The marking of servants had continued during the English Civil War, but the more complete emergence of a uniform comes with the greater assertion of central authority following this era of discord. Even officers, who during the English Civil War had worn their own choice of civilian clothes, were expected to present a more uniform appearance in the period afterwards. In 1686, the Earl of Oxford specified: 'All the Captains coats are to be of blue cloth faced with the same, the lace of the said coats to be of gold, laid double upon every seam and slits with a gold foot between the two laces. The buttons of gold thread with a gold fringe round the sleeves, under which must be laid the same lace as down the seams.'[2]

The materials might be more sumptious, but the degree of control is exactly the same as that imposed on the common soldier. The message of this re-assertion of authority would not have been lost on the population at large as until the late 17th century, the wearing of a complete uniform, from top to toe, was a sign of subservience. A century earlier in France, a group of pioneers, that is, military labourers, were presented to the royal army by a wealthy merchant. 'Each one was attired and arrayed in red caps', records the receipt of delivery, 'and cassocks and hose of green woollen cloth with two white crosses and the first and last letters of the name of their election sewn on the front and back of their garments.'[3] None of the soldiers in the service of the French king at this time wore a uniform and the clear purpose of this elaborate outfit was to mark these forced labourers as the property of the king and to inhibit them from escaping or mingling with the soldiers. Galley slaves at the same time also wore uniforms. Indeed, the pioneers might well have been prisoners given the opportunity of military service.

Musketeer illustrated in Jacob de Gheyn's *Manual of Arms* published in 1607. This highly influential manual detailed the drill of soldiers fighting under the Dutch system and is the beginning of a whole series of volumes exerting greater control and discipline over the waging of warfare.

His clothes, however, are far from ordered and represent the typical civilian style of clothes worn by most soldiers into battle in the early and middle 17th century.

Recreated unit of pikemen from the English Civil War. They represent the Fairfax Battalia fighting on the side of the Parliamentarians, but the clothes they wear could have been worn by either side, their being no set uniform in this period. Red and blue were the cheapest and most widely available dyes at the time.

Uniformity in the 16th century was dismissed as most unwarlike. The Duke of Alba, the great Spanish warlord, believed that 10,000 soldiers boldly clad in different colours according to their personal tastes looked more menacing than 20,000 men all dressed in black 'as if they were townsmen and shopkeepers'.[4] Hence the fashion among German *Landsknecht* mercenaries, some of the most feared professional soldiers at that time, for clothes that were a riot of different colours and materials, all thrown together as though exploding out of a wardrobe. A century later, rulers and their subjects were tired of war and more than happy to see such independent marauders reduced to the status of identical servants.

But it was more than just a desire for order that led to the creation of uniforms. Indeed, the occurrence of uniforms in the late 17th century and the sense of political and social order they brought can be said to be a coincidental by-product of more important economic changes. An army of individuals clad in any clothes they desired was ultimately one that clothed itself at its own cost with little expense demanded of its commander or government. An army that has to be clothed in identical uniforms and equipment is very expensive and it was only, ironically, after a century of European civil wars that an economic structure had evolved which enabled kings and governments to clothe their soldiers in uniforms at a more reasonable cost.

At the beginning of the 17th century, the cost of supplying thousands of men with standardised equipment was prohibitive, but as the period of war progressed and the size of armies grew larger, merchants were able to strike cost-effective deals with generals as their workers were geared up for producing long runs of similar clothing and they could make bigger purchases of raw materials at a discounted rate. A little indication of the subsequent 17th century boom in military trade is provided by the record of imported dyes into Bristol. Between 1613 and 1655, approximately 17,500lb of madder arrived from Amsterdam, enough to dye red 58,000 coats a year. From the West Indies, the importation of indigo into Bristol rose from 224lb in 1613 to 11,816lb in 1655 when the majority of West Country soldiers wore blue uniforms.[5] Oliver Cromwell's New Model Army realised the value of an efficient relationship with their suppliers and military tradesmen flourished as a result. In 1646, 13 London shoemakers signed contracts to deliver 8000 pairs of shoes 'of good neat leather'. Precisely four weeks later the shoes were delivered and they were paid in full.[6] By the time peace came, wartime merchants were keen to carry on supplying military buyers, offering them increasingly reasonable deals as they competed with each other for a diminishing market. Indeed, commanders of regiments had now learned to pass the expense of providing uniforms onto their soldiers who were expected to pay for their clothes out of their own wages. In the British Army this payment was called 'off reckonings' and persisted for many years, enabling colonels to fiddle their regimental expenses. Thus everyone gained from this new industry and the uniformed soldier was born.

As the political, social and economic virtues of uniformed soldiers continued to be appreciated towards the end of the 17th century, so a new layer of meaning was added to a soldier's uniform clothing. Nations at peace with themselves with booming mercantile economies could now set about building national armies that could be used to engage in wars of conquest and influence around the world. It is in the 18th century that we see the full development of military uniforms and the full exploitation of the fact that a uniformed army was a disciplined army not only at home but also abroad and as such could win decisively on any battlefield.

Trooper of the Tangier Horse raised by Charles II in 1661 to garrison the colony of Tangier he inherited from his Portuguese wife. These soldiers returned to England in 1683 to become part of the Royal Regiment of Dragoons. The trooper wears the red jacket typical of royal cavalry after the Restoration.

French grenadier of the late 17th century, from a print by Goichon. This soldier wears the civilian fashion typical of the period. It was under Louis XIV in the 1660s that uniforms were introduced into the French army.

DISCIPLINE OF ARMIES

The one big lesson of warfare to emerge out of the century of civil wars in Europe in the 16th and 17th centuries was that discipline and order among soldiers won battles. Again and again, military writers during this period emphasise its tactical importance. Francisco de Valdes, a Spanish veteran of the wars against the Protestants, concluded: 'that Armie which is best ordered, though it be least in number of men, shall always (according to reason) become victorious,'[7] This view was further enhanced by the belief that battlefield discipline was responsible for the great victories of the ancient world. As Machiavelli put it: 'The Romans... made light of dangers since their discipline was good; and, since they did not despair of victory, they remained firm and dogged, and fought with the same courage and the same virtu at the end as at the start,' adding, 'good discipline stimulates courage'.[8] The decisive battlefield victories of commanders such as Oliver Cromwell and Gustavus Adolphus, renowned for leading strongly controlled armies, meant that this view became the primary military doctrine for all Western European armies.

The need for discipline on the battlefield was matched by a plethora of drill books, exercises and rules which the successful military commander was expected to enforce on his troops. This drive towards greater control had its visual expression in a progressive tightening of the rules and orders regarding uniforms. In the late 17th century, the government might specify the overall colour and items of a uniform, but the details of lining colour and other particulars were left to the commander in charge of his regiment. Lord Chesterfield records in 1667: 'The soldiers red coats lined with black and black flags with a red cross in a black field, which I did, because I was at that time in mourning for my mother.'[9]

By the beginning of the 18th century, faced with a major continental war to win, the Duke of Marlborough, commander of British forces, imposed greater control over the purchase and design of uniforms by having the Office of the Controller of Army Pay Accounts created by Letters Patent in 1703. Marlborough's *Instructions* declared that 'the General [Marlborough] having approved and sealed the patterns for clothing, the Colonels are to contract for its supply and exhibit to the Controllers the contracts, which must specify the qualities, quantities and prices of each

Prussian musketeer, fusilier and grenadier of 1787 showing the increased rigidity of uniforms towards the end of the century, including the use of the stock around the neck to keep the head up and the white crossbelts used to support equipment despite putting pressure on the chest.

Prussian infantry of 1700. A grenadier (left) and two musketeers wear the dark blue jackets that became associated with the Prussian army in the 18th century. So popular were uniforms in the German states that Frederick the Great of Prussia always wore his dark blue jacket whatever the occasion.

particular. The Colonels or their agents are to exhibit to the Controllers the debt owing to off-reckonings (money deducted from a soldier's pay to cover his clothing) on Feb. 24, 1703. In England the Controllers are to take care that the clothes for the army are furnished according to contract, abroad a certificate to this effect is to be rendered by the Captain-General or his deputy, and they are to see that the clothing does not exceed in cost the amount of off-reckonings. Having satisfied themselves on these points, the Controllers are to certify the Paymaster, who in absence of this certificate, is not to part with the off-reckonings and where regiments are in debt they are to see that it is gradually reduced.'[10]

Having gained control over uniform finances, a further step was taken by the British Army in 1707 with a Royal Warrant establishing a Board of General Officers to check the quality of soldiers clothing bought by the colonels of each regiment. Potential manufacturers were to supply samples of their clothing which would then be checked against standard patterns, that is, already accepted uniform archetypes, kept in the office of the Controller of Army accounts in Whitehall. If passed by the Board of Officers, these samples would then be sealed and the completed contract of uniforms compared with the agreed patterns. Colonels in their turn would have to demonstrate that they could afford to pay for the desired quality of clothing and they would not be allowed to inspect their own order.

To help regimental commanders and their suppliers meet the exacting demands imposed by government, a series of clothing Regulations books were published in Britain throughout the 18th century. The *Cloathing Book* of 1742 details everything a soldier should wear including the colour of his facings (that is, the lining that showed on the lapels and cuffs of his jacket) and the shape of the lace appearing on his sleeve. 4th Barrell's Regiment, for example, should wear blue facings, white lace with blue zig-zag, square button loops and ladder pattern on sleeve, whereas 3rd Howard's Regiment had light buff facings, white lace with yellow line and red chain, and square button loops with herringbone arrangement on the sleeve. Officers were expected to wear uniforms similar to their men and these too were controlled by regulation.

The same desire for regulation and standardisation swept across Western Europe. National armies began to be associated with the colours of their uniform. If England wore red,

Birth of the Thin Red Line.
An English platoon about to let loose a volley of disciplined musket fire at charging Scots Jacobite warriors at the battle of Killiecrankie in 1689. Ironically, on this occasion the use of disciplined firepower failed to stop the Highland charge and the resulting defeat led in part to the introduction of the socket bayonet. The appearance of a complete uniform, however, is clear. The red coat is worn with yellow cuffs and breeches representing Colonel Hasting's Regiment. A cartridge box is slung over the shoulder and a plug bayonet and powder horn hang from the belt. Painting by Richard Hook.

then France had Bourbon white derived from the royal flag. The various German states came into line with light blue for Bavaria, red for Saxony, and dark blue for Prussia. Austria wore the pearl-grey of undyed wool, while Russia left behind the various colours of its quasi-Asian army to position itself closer to the West with a dark green coat. This fashion for national colours stopped at the Turkish border, thus confirming the essentially Western European character of uniforms and their association with a warfare of discipline and order.

That the wearing of national colours did not always help in the identification of soldiers in the smoke and chaos of the battle is proved by the French Colonel de la Colonie at Schellenberg Heights in 1704, in which white-coated Frenchmen confronted Austrians in pearl-grey: 'I became aware of several lines of infantry in greyish-white uniforms on our left flank. I verily believed reinforcements had reached us... So, in the error I laboured under I shouted to my men that they were Frenchmen and friends. Having, however, made a closer inspection, I discovered bunches of straw attached to their standards, badges the enemy are in the custom of wearing in battle, but at that very moment was struck in the jaw by a ball that stupified me.'[11] The Austrians did not seek to avoid this confusion either, as their soldiers were expected to whiten the raw wool of their coats with pipeclay, making them look even more like French soldiers. The point should not be forgotten that coloured uniforms were there not to distinguish the enemy, but to show to whom the common soldier belonged. Colour as a badge of service remained useful in the 18th century as armies stretched to meet imperial demands and had to rely increasingly on enforced recruitment with many soldiers being regarded as little more than prisoners with guns.

The degree of servitude represented by a uniform in the 18th century is best exemplified by the introduction of the stock. A black strip of leather, the stock was secured around the neck of the ordinary soldier with the intention of keeping his head up and presenting a smart appearance around the collar of his jacket. Tales of this reviled collar emphasise its demeaning, constrictive aspects. Colonel Robertson in his reminiscences of life in the British Army in India in the early 19th century recalls an incident before the battle of Mudki: 'Colonel Bolton [Robertson's commander at the time] was a fine old soldier, but very strict, and still adhered to ancient ways and customs. In those days the

Discipline of Armies caricatured in a late 18th century English cartoon. Ragged recruits found in a pub, possibly drunk as they take the King's shilling, are lined up before a ramrod straight officer in meticulous uniform wearing a stock round his neck.

men had to wear high and stiff leather stocks to keep their heads up, about as absurd an article as can be imagined for a man to fight in. On this occasion he, the Colonel, was quite wild at the straggling of the men... and he observed one of them with his stock off. "What do you mean, sir?" he said. "Put on your stock immediately." I was standing close to the man, and observed a wild expression come over his worn face. For a moment I thought he was going to shoot the Colonel; then he put his forehead on the muzzle of his firelock, and blew his brains out. I don't know how the Colonel felt, but it gave me a very ugly turn.'[12] Colonel Bolton, it appears, was more of an 18th century-style commander, having served in the Peninsular War against Napoleon's Army, whereas Robertson, then a subaltern, belonged to a later, more relaxed generation. In camp, Robertson was known to walk around with a ten foot boa-constrictor, rather than a stock, hanging around his neck.

The authoritarian aspect of the leather stock is enhanced when one discovers that officers were let off with a soft stock made out of black cloth or silk. This view, however, is contradicted by several contemporary accounts emphasising the practicality of the item and how it need not be made of leather. Bennett Cuthbertson praises the stock in his 1768 *System for the Compleat Interior Management and Oeconomy of a Battalion of Infantry*: 'Black stocks, besides having a more soldierly appearance than white ones, are a saving to the men in point of washing, and do not shew the dirt of a shirt, so much after a day's wear: two will be necessary for each man; one of horse-hair for common use; the other of Manchester velvet for dress: and it will contribute much to the smartness of both, to edge them with scarlet cloth: the each for the clasps to fix in, are best of leather, as that will last while the stocks do.'[13] A more common sense tone was also set by the 1795 *Regulations for the use of His Majesty's Troops, upon their arrival in the West Indies:* 'the stocks should be made of black cloth in preference to leather, as better adapted to a warm climate.'[14] Ultimately, the purpose of the stock was one of smartness, not unlike the use of a tie with a business suit, and it proved popular in its soft form in civilian fashion. King George IV popularised it with his own version in 1822, the 'Royal George' made out of black velvet with a satin bow.

The process of military regimentation and order reached its culmination in the late 18th century. In the British Army,

the use of facings and different shaped lace to differentiate units was enhanced by the introduction of buttons and shoulder-belt plates bearing the number or devices of a regiment, including the royal crown. Inevitably this created a sense of belonging and the army encouraged this esprit de corps by adding the names of victorious battles in which a unit had fought to the metal plates of its caps or helmets. Early in the 18th century, rank had been relatively easy to determine by the cut and richness of an officer's clothing compared to an ordinary soldier, but as standardisation reduced this difference, so new methods of rank identification were introduced. A crimson sash was worn across the chest and a gorget, a little engraved metal plate, suspended around the neck. On an officer's jacket, gold and silver lace was used, but after 1768 metallic shoulder knots developed into fringed epaulettes of metallic cord secured to the shoulder. These were further elaborated with 'wings' of gilded chain. In 1795, a system of chevrons worn on the sleeve (two for a corporal, three for a sergeant) was introduced to distinguish non-commissioned officers in the cavalry and this was extended to the rest of the army in 1802. Many of the changes in clothing throughout this period appeared at regimental level first and were then accepted throughout the army, rather than being originated from above, but despite being open to experimentation it was important that the government maintained the overall right

Temple Bar & St. Paul's Volunteer demonstrating Present Arms, 1st Motion, painted by Thomas Rowlandson, 1798. Soldiering became increasingly popular during Britain's war against Napoleon and a number of privately raised units of volunteers helped swell **the number of men under arms, all of them privately equipped. This soldier wears the Tarleton helmet introduced for light infantry during the war against America in the 1780s, consisting of a leather skull with a coloured turban and plumes.**

to control the appearance of its soldiers.

By the middle of the 18th century, uniforms had become more than just a mark of submission, it being believed that the regimentation of men in identical uniforms aided the accomplishment of the complex drill and manouevres that had to be mastered to create the discipline essential for victory in battle. Some monarchs took this concept one step further, convinced that the discipline of uniforms could be applied to civil administration as well. Frederick the Great, as head of the German state of Prussia, always wore the undress uniform of the first battallion of his Guard, and he instructed many of his civil servants to wear uniforms as well. Joseph II of Austria, ever impressed by Frederick, followed suit and was constantly surrounded by his uniformed Imperial Guard. That this regularity appealed enormously to the German mind, more attuned to order than most, was demonstrated by the spread of military fashion to German male civil costume by the middle of the 18th century when 'coats, waistcoats and sleeves were gradually reduced in length... in strict accordance with changes in the clothing of Prussian soldiers. Around 1750 German gentlemen began to adopt the Prussian army custom of wearing a wig with a pigtail, the *Zopfzeit*.'[15] This militarisation of society was not welcomed by either France or Britain who preferred to see a decrease in the role of the military, an attitude that would suddenly be reversed in the Napoleonic Wars at the end of the century.

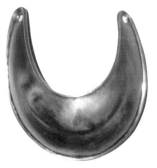

Top, British officer's gorget, late 18th century. This little metal plate was worn suspended from ribbon around the neck and served as a badge of rank.

Above, soldiers of the 10th Light Dragoons, painted by George Stubbs, 1793. King George III appointed his son, the Prince of Wales, Colonel Commandant of the Regiment and it subsequently became popular among the fashionable. The celebrated dandy Beau

Brummell served as a captain, although he later resigned on the grounds that it was moving its base to Manchester. The painting records one of the earliest uses of sleeve chevrons to denote rank, later employed throughout the army.

BRITISH SCARLET

The red coat of the British soldier in the 18th century was to become as much a part of the identity of the new British nation, established in 1707 with the Act of Union, as the Union Jack flag or the constitutional monarchy, but it could so easily have been blue. In the chaos of the English Civil War, a century earlier, both blue and red dyes were imported in large quantities for the jackets of soldiers on both sides. Because of their wide availability, this made them a cheap and favourite pigment for military clothes, their dyeing process also just involving one stage whereas other colours, mixing dyes, involved two stages. Grey was the only other contender for cheap British uniform colouring as this was made of undyed wool.

Both Parliamentarians and Royalists wore red, blue and grey jackets, preferring to depend on the colour of their sashes or plumes to distinguish one from the other. Cromwell's victorious New Model Army was renowned for wearing a uniform consisting of a red jacket and this set a precedent for the army of the government wearing red coats, a report of 1645 declaring that the whole army are 'Red-coats'.[16] Units within the New Model Army were distinguished by the use of different colour facings, that is, the linings of their clothes that showed such as collars or cuffs, a tradition of regimental identification which continued into the British Army of the 18th century. With the restoration of the monarchy in 1660, one of its oldest established regiments, the Horse Guards, was clad in red jackets faced with blue, but another regiment known as the Earl of Oxford's Horse and made up of ex-Cromwellian cavalry troops wore a uniform of blue faced with red. Red was not to be treated as a national colour, but just one among many, including green, yellow, and grey, indicating particular regiments. It must be remembered that as it was the individual commanders of regiments who were responsible for their clothing then both personal taste and whatever cloth was available at a good price could be just as a strong a determinent of an early uniform's appearance.

With the accession of William III, a Dutch candidate for the English throne, blue became a fashionable colour for officers' jackets, as indicated in the earliest recorded uniform code for officers laid down by the Earl of Oxford in 1686: 'all the Captains coats are to be of blue cloth faced with the same, the lace of the said coats to be of gold...'.[17]

Regimental coat worn by Lt. Colonel John Dalgleish of the 21st Regiment of Foot, the Royal North British Fuzileers, around 1780 while serving in the war against the American colonies. Based on regulations of 1768, the coat differs from the standard pattern by having a raised collar. It is made from scarlet woolen cloth with dark blue regimental facings. The body is lined with white shalloon and the coat-tail turnbacks with white cassimere.

Such a relaxed state of affairs was acceptable in a time of relative peace, when only minor colonial campaigns were being fought, but when Britain entered a major continental war in the early 18th century under the guidance of the Duke of Marlborough, then a need for standardisation was clear. In 1702, Marlborough ordered that his 'officers be all clothed in red, plain and uniform, which is expected they shall wear on all marches and other duties as well as days of Review.'[18] Thus, the need for discipline and group identity among an army at war against a major continental opponent meant that a national colour must be chosen and for England this became red. Not only was it a cheap dye, having been used widely throughout the 17th century, but it also had the good fortune of coinciding with the red cross of St. George, the patron saint of England since the Middle Ages.

St. George, venerated as a patron saint of soldiers since early Christian times, appears to have first become popular among European knights fighting as Crusaders in the Near East from the 11th century onwards. Associated with a red cross against a white background, St. George was later adopted as a national saint in England in the 14th century and with this his emblem becomes a national badge.

Detail of sleeve cuff on Dalgleish jacket showing gilded buttons bearing the regimental number and the crown of King George III, ultimate commander of the regiment and army.

Detail of embroidered thistle turnback ornament on the coat-tails of the rear of the Dalgleish jacket.

Previous to this, there is evidence that Edward I in his Welsh campaign of the late 13th century identified his footsoldiers with armbands bearing the red cross of St. George. White tunics generally became a useful way of identifying certain specialist and perhaps unreliable elements in a medieval army and red crosses could be sewn to these for further proof of identity. During his war in France, King Henry V ordered that 'every man of what estate or condition that he be, of our party, bear a band of St. George',[19] and as this move coincided with one of England's greatest victories over the French at Agincourt in 1415, it is little wonder that in the same year, the English church should see to it that St. George's Day became a festival of the highest rank.

From this moment on, a national badge had been confirmed and the red cross of St. George continued to be worn throughout the 15th and 16th centuries, becoming the basis of the United Kingdom's national flag in the 17th century when James VI of Scotland became James I of England and the white diagonal cross of St. Andrew on a blue background (Scotland's flag) was combined with the red cross of St. George on a white background (England's flag), thus producing the first version of the Union Jack flag. This symbolic process of political union was completed in 1800 when the red diagonal cross of St. Patrick and Ireland was added to the Union Jack. It was, however, the red cross of St. George that continued to be the most dominant element in this standard and this served only to strengthen the presence of red as the core national colour and thus a colour most suitable for the national British Army uniform. By the 19th century, the sense that red was the national colour above all others was consolidated by its widespread use in popular culture, including being the colour chosen to represent the British Empire in countless maps and atlases and being a useful shorthand for British troops in such popular images as the Thin Red Line.

Classic British redcoat who would have fought at the battle of Waterloo in 1815. A battalion soldier of the 69th Foot, he wears a short scarlet jacket, grey trousers, stock around his neck, and white crossbelts to support his equipment. His 1812 pattern Belgic shako is covered with a leather covering to protect it against the rain.

Opposite, **detail of epaulette worn on shoulder of Dalgleish jacket to denote officer rank and bearing the regimental insignia of a thistle. The epaulette fringe is made of gold bullion, very fine gold wire twisted around a core thread.**

The Thin Red Line painted by Robert Gibb in 1881. It depicts the 93rd Highlanders stopping an attack by Russian cavalry at the battle of Balaklava in 1854 during the Crimean War, and was inspired by the war correspondent of *The Times*, William Russell, who originally described the combatants as a 'Thin Red Streak'. It rapidly became a Victorian icon of British military courage in the face of overwhelming odds, consolidating red as the martial colour of the nation. Ironically, within twenty years of this painting being finished, scarlet was replaced by khaki as the army service colour.

SPECIALISATION

Specialisation in troop tasks had already occurred in the 17th century with the presence of musketeers, pikemen and dragoons serving in separate units, each carrying their own special weapons and equipment, but generally speaking they still wore the same basic clothes. By the late 17th century this process had begun to be reflected in different types of uniforms. One of the first of these specialist units to be thus identified were the grenadiers. Taking their name from the primitive hand grenades they carried in a pouch slung over their shoulders, they soon evolved into an elite group of soldiers, attracting some of the tallest and most fiercesome warriors in the regular army. This largely derived from the fact that the effective throwing of hand grenades required great physical strength as well as courage, for grenadiers were placed at the forefront of an army within short range of the enemy.

In his diary entry of June 1678, John Evelyn gives us a very early description of the new grenadier uniform style: 'furred caps with coped crowns like Janizaries, which gave them a fierce expression: while some wore long hoods hanging down behind, as fools are pictured. Their clothing was piebald, yellow and red.' They wore caps rather than helmets or hats, it was believed, because this gave them greater freedom for hanging their muskets over their shoulders on a sling and throwing their hand grenades, but the mere practicality of this item was overtaken by its development into a badge of distinction and an emblem of physical height and strength with the soft fisherman's stocking cap (Evelyn's fools hood) being displaced by the tall crowned, stiff fronted embroidered mitre, often with a rim of fur around it. Whether this headwear was directly inspired by similar tall hats worn by Turkish Janissaries is unknown and it soon became an item of its own style and tradition. In the 18th century in the British Army, the grenadier cap lost its fur and acquired a brass plate with the regiment's insignia or number engraved on it. Among continental armies, however, the fur remained, becoming the dominant feature until it evolved into the bearskin, a fur domed front with brass plate to indicate regiment and a soft cap crown hanging down behind. This was worn by the leading regiments of French, Austrian, and German armies, the most famous being Napoleon's bearskin clad Imperial Guard.

Recreated British grenadier's cap of the 17th Foot, c.1759. The regimental emblem and motto is surmounted by the Latin initials of King George and his crown.

Spanish grenadiers in Hamburg in 1807 wearing elaborate fur-rimmed caps with embroidered cloth hanging hoods or 'bags'. Fur caps for grenadiers were much more popular in continental Europe than Britain throughout the 18th and early 19th centuries.

During the Napoleonic Wars, the British grenadiers of the Foot Guards wore the same shako-style hats worn by the rest of the army, but with the defeat of Napoleon, more continental styles were allowed and the Prince Regent proclaimed, just one month after the battle of Waterloo in 1815, that the First Foot Guards, the premier infantry unit of the British Army, be 'made a Regiment of Grenadiers and be styled the First or Grenadier Regiment of Foot Guards in commemoration of having defeated the Grenadiers of the French Imperial Guards', Napoleon's elite fur-capped troops. Thus it was that the bearskin entered the British Army as a token of victory and became the classic item of headwear worn by the Foot Guards who continue to wear it today when guarding the Queen at Buckingham Palace and on all ceremonial occasions. As an item worn in battle, the bearskin continued until the Crimean War in 1854 when the demands of a tough campaign saw it replaced in battle by simple sealskin caps. British bearskins have always been made from the skins of black bears from Canada and Russia, but today these skins are supplied from culled animals and not hunted specifically for bearskin caps. An officer's bearskin is eleven and a half inches tall, taller than the nine inches worn by all other ranks.

Prussian grenadier and grenadier officer, c.1815, wearing large brass cap plates bearing their regimental insignia.

Regimental Quartermaster-Sergeant of the 23rd Royal Welch Fusiliers in 1833 painted by A.J. Dubois-Drahonet. He wears the massive bearskin grenadier cap introduced into the British Army in recognition of the defeat of Napoleon's grenadiers at the battle of Waterloo in 1815.

British Grenadier Guards on parade at Windsor Castle, the Royal Residence of the Queen. They still wear the bearskin cap, adopted almost two hundred years previously, but carry the new L85A1 5.56mm rifle, symbolising the fact that despite being present for ceremonial duties they are also part of the current British fighting force.

WILD MEN

By the middle of the 18th century, European governments had tamed the wilder instincts of the warrior that had made the previous century such a nightmare of chaos and military excess. Through creating, regimented, uniformed lines of soldiers, most European nations now possessed the power not only to solve any internal conflicts they might face, but also to turn outwards, to contest areas of influence beyond their own frontiers. It was in these wars of conquest and empire, that European powers found themselves in the unique situation of appearing more effective, more advanced, more civilised, than many of their opponents. They had put their own tribal wars behind them – their wars of raging mobs charging wildly at each other – and exchanged them for wars conducted by rules, instructions, and, above all, discipline.

The European uniformed soldier of the 18th century appeared to be somewhat superior to the Celtic clansman, the Tatar horseman and the rebel African slave. And yet, as the uniformed soldiers waited in their lines to deliver a devastating volley of musketry at the primitive warriors rushing blindly towards them, there was still something impressive, still frightening, still dynamic about this primeval onrush of individuals, all imbued with the strength of deep and aggressive warrior cultures – and sometimes, despite the uniforms and the co-ordinated volley – the primeval charge would unnerve that European discipline and the primitive warriors would smash the carefully arranged units to pieces. Despite the proven advantages of civilisation in warfare, there was still a place for the dark, untamed wild man.

In Britain, the Celtic dominion of Scotland had been formally annexed by the Act of Union in 1707, but factions opposed to this continued to lead rebellions and their chief source of military power were the clansmen of the Scottish Highlands. These clansmen fought in the old Celtic way of tribal headmen leading warriors armed with shields and swords in a blood-curdling charge. They wore no uniform and effected no complex manouevres. They had mastered the use of musketry, but this was second to their use of the Highland charge. And frequently, they were successful, despite being up against one of the most sophisticated of European military powers. In the last great rebellion of 1745, the British army of redcoats was devastated at Prestonpans, the Highland charge broke their disciplined lines, and Celtic clansmen threatened to march on London. In the following year, the British army returned to Scotland and this time stood their ground at Culloden, where artillery and lines of musketry brought the Highland charge to a halt. The last great Celtic rebellion was over, but the British had learned a valuable lesson.

The English had recruited Scots soldiers since the early 17th century, but these had been largely from the anglicised lowlands and when they were uniformed, they wore the same outfit as their English comrades. In the early 18th century, following rebel successes, the British government turned to the Highlanders themselves and assembled a police force of clansmen to patrol the wild lands beyond the border. An English order of 1725 describes their dress at the time: 'The officers commanding companies take care to provide a plaid clothing and bonnet in the Highland dress for the non-commissioned officers and soldiers, belonging to their companies, the plaid of each company to be as near as they can of the same sort of colour; that besides the plaid clothing, to be furnished each year, each soldier is to receive from his captain a pair of brogues every six weeks, a pair of stockings every three months, a shirt and cravat every six months.'[21] A further measure introduced to give some discipline to these warriors is suggested by an order

Early Highland warriors in British service in 1744 from Grose's _Military Antiquities_. They wear the original form of the tartan plaid which wrapped around the shoulder, serving as a cloak, kilt and blanket.

allocating each a number which may well have been provided as an identity badge. During the Jacobite uprising of 1745, loyalist Highlanders each wore the red cross of St. George on their bonnet. The plaid described above, the *breacan-an-fheilidh*, was a traditional Highland combination of kilt and cloak made from a 12 yard length of tartan cloth. The lower part of this was secured around the waist to form the kilt while the rest was slung over the shoulder. The more familiar pleated kilt, or little kilt, *fheilidh beg*, began as an item of undress uniform, developing later into the standard British Highland outfit.

In 1739, these Independent Companies were brought together to form the oldest of the British Highland Regiments, called the Black Watch. Although now part of the British Army, these clansmen were not forced to wear the standard British uniform, but were allowed to wear their traditional Celtic dress, although the disparate local tartans were standardised into one dark green and black pattern

Black Watch and Gordon Highlanders of 1812 drawn by Charles Hamilton-Smith. They wear British scarlet jackets on top of their dark green Highland tartan kilts with sporrans.

Sergeant and private of the 92nd Gordon Highlanders photographed by Hill and Adamson c.1858. The sergeant on the left wears a shell jacket, typical of undress uniform at this time in the British Army. The private wears full dress uniform including the massive Highland bonnet made of a wire cage clad in ostrich feathers dyed black.

Scottish Regiments of the British Army in 1895, painted by Simkin for *The Boy's Own Paper*.
Front rank, left to right:
Seaforth Highlanders, corporal and piper; Royal Scots, Queen's Own Cameron Highlanders, private and sergeant; The Cameronians, officer; Black Watch, officer; Highland Light Infantry, officer; Princess Louise's Argyll and Sutherland Highlanders, officer; Royal Scots Fusiliers, officer; Princess Louise's Argyll and Sutherland Highlanders, piper; Scots Gards, private; Gordon Highlanders, private; The King's Own Scottish Borderers, colour-sergeant; The Black Watch, drummer.
Rear rank, left to right:
2nd Dragoons, Royal Scots Greys, trooper; Queen's Own Cameron Highlanders, field-officer; Gordon Highlanders, field-officer; 2nd Dragoons, Royal Scots Greys, officer.

known as Government Tartan. The important point was that though they were now part of the British Army, the native aggression and ferocity that so impressed the British was not be ironed out and this was symbolised by these warriors being allowed to wear, beneath their red jacket, their traditional kilt alongside other Celtic attributes such as the sporran and tartan stockings.

In 1743, the Black Watch were ordered out of Scotland and marched to London, but such was the mistrust and fear of these Highland troops for this foreign land, many of them still only speaking their native Gaelic, that a number of them promptly deserted and their ringleaders had to be executed. After Culloden, the recruitment of Highland warriors increased with the raising of such famous regiments as the Seaforth Highlanders, the Cameron Highlanders, the Argyllshire Highlanders and the Sutherland Highlanders, all of them wearing tartan kilts based on the old dark green and black sett of the Government Tartan. Some of these regiments were raised by Scots landowners who had previously supported rebellions against the government and now sought to prove their loyalty. Interestingly, the older Scots regiments raised in the 17th century, termed Lowlanders, did not wear kilts or tartan, although by the end of the 19th century under the pressure of fashion and the illustrious performance of their Highland colleagues, they were allowed to wear tartan trews and their pipers to wear kilts. The tartan chosen for several of these Lowland regiments was the Royal Stewart, a red-based pattern, thus indicating their closeness to British Royalty and their separateness from the original Highlanders.

By the late 18th century, the British experiment was seen to have worked with magnificent results. Kilted Highland regiments retained their Celtic talent for battlefield ferocity, and despite being armed with muskets and regimented in lines, were eager to let go with a Highland charge – much to the approval of their British commanders. At the battle of Fontenoy, the front ranks of the 43rd Regiment of Foot Highlanders discharged their muskets, then rushed the French with their broadswords, Sergeant James Campbell winning great renown for killing nine Frenchmen with his sword before having his arm blown off by a cannonball as he was trying to kill his tenth. Outside Quebec, on the Plains of Abraham in 1759, charging British Highlanders completed the rout of the French – a victory that secured

Canada for the British Empire. 'When these highlanders took to their broadswords, my god!' noted an observer. 'What a havoc they made! They drove everything before them, and walls could not resist their fury.' In 1766, a proud William Pitt the Elder declared: 'I found... in the mountains of the North... a hardy and intrepid race of men... they served with fidelity as they fought with valour, and conquered for you in every part of the world.'[22]

Highland regiments continued to serve the British Army in the 19th and 20th centuries wearing their traditional costume, although sometimes the rigours of campaigning did not suit the kilt. At the battle of Vitoria during the Peninsular War, the 92nd had to cross ditches infested with thorns and briars which tore at their naked legs, the Gordon Highlanders being ordered to swap their kilts for pantaloons. In the First World War, Highland regiments wore tartan kilts into battle but these were later disguised with khaki aprons. By the Second World War, standard battledress trousers predominated, although photographs sometimes show Highlanders wearing kilts in battle contrary to orders, the Celtic spirit of the wild men proving impossible to subdue completely.

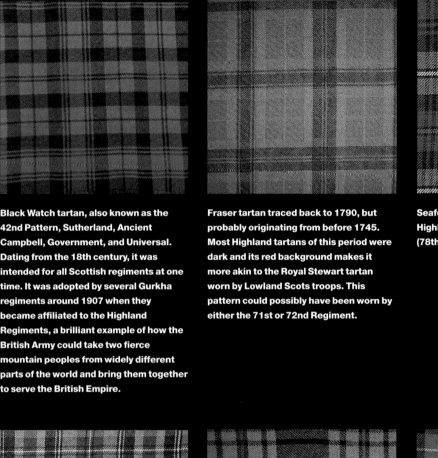

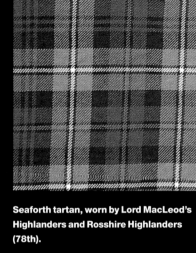

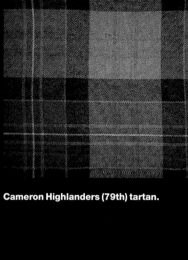

Black Watch tartan, also known as the 42nd Pattern, Sutherland, Ancient Campbell, Government, and Universal. Dating from the 18th century, it was intended for all Scottish regiments at one time. It was adopted by several Gurkha regiments around 1907 when they became affiliated to the Highland Regiments, a brilliant example of how the British Army could take two fierce mountain peoples from widely different parts of the world and bring them together to serve the British Empire.

Fraser tartan traced back to 1790, but probably originating from before 1745. Most Highland tartans of this period were dark and its red background makes it more akin to the Royal Stewart tartan worn by Lowland Scots troops. This pattern could possibly have been worn by either the 71st or 72nd Regiment.

Seaforth tartan, worn by Lord MacLeod's Highlanders and Rosshire Highlanders (78th).

Cameron Highlanders (79th) tartan.

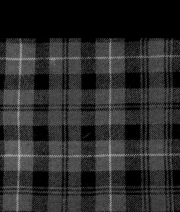

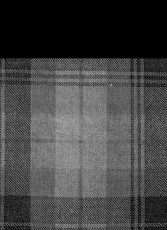

Prince Charles Stuart's tartan, adopted by the 72nd Regiment for officers' trews in 1823.

Tartan designed in 1907 for Pipers' plaids of the Gurkha Rifles. Known as Childers pattern, after the War Minister, it was intended for non-Scottish soldiers, including English, who could not lay claim

Tartan for Drummers' plaids of the 92nd Regiment, c.1795.

Tartan for Bandsmens' and Musicians' plaids of the 42nd Regiment.

Hungarian horsemen from Jost Amman's *Kunstbuchlin* of 1599. The horseman on the left wears the Turkish-style kaftan with frogging loops which became the model for the dolman of the Hussar uniform. The horseman on the right wears a fur trimmed cloak, the model for the pelisse worn by Hussars over their shoulders.

BALKAN BANDITS

Elsewhere in Europe in the 18th century, a similar process of absorbing the wilder elements encountered in frontier warfare was enacted and by doing so added a new dimension to the meaning of uniforms. In central Europe, since the 15th century, a long period of almost continuous warfare had ebbed and flowed where the German and Slavic states bordered the Turkish Ottoman Empire. Occasionally, there might be a major campaign or battle, but for most of the time the frontier was plagued by low-intensity warfare of an awful kind in which raid and counter-raid followed each other endlessly, ethnic and religious hatred provoked merciless atrocities, and young men saw their only future employment as armed brigands, looting and ravaging neighbouring lands.

When a major campaign did occur, these freelance border warriors were easily recruited into either side where, because of their native fixation on loot and easy prey, they could not be depended on to serve as disciplined, regular cavalry, but were instead expected to carry on their livelihood as mounted bandits, ranging across enemy territory, burning villages and crops, terrorising civilians, and, occasionally, gathering information. In the 16th century, Ogier Ghiselin de Busbecq, a German ambassador at Constantinople, was warned of these maurauders on his way through the Balkans and preferred to travel by river. Even Suleyman the Magnificent, the Turkish Sultan, complained to him about them: 'What has been the good of having made peace here, if they are going to disturb it and continue to fight?'[23] The problem was that these warriors knew no other way of life. Busbecq calls them Heydons. In Hungary, they were called Hussars.

The costume worn by these light irregular cavalry was highly distinctive and set a style adopted by all later Hussar regiments throughout Europe over the next four centuries. In the 16th century, the basic elements consisted of a loose tunic buttoned with horizontal lines of frogging (ornamental loops of braid or cord), a stocking cap with a fur band, a fur cloak, a sash or belt, breeches and brightly coloured boots. Feathers could be an additional decoration to the animal furs, indicating the dual origin of these horsemen as hunters as well as bandits. They fought with curved sabres, bows and arrows, and firearms. This outfit was similar to that worn by other Eurasian warrior peoples whose livelihood depended on raiding and one can follow this style of dress and life from the Balkans across the Black Sea to the Caucasus and Central Asia where the Cossacks and Tatars operated. The characteristic tunic frogging worn by all these warrior peoples can be seen on Ottoman Turkish kaftans of the 15th and 16th centuries and this is likely to be the ultimate origin of the style.

The similarity of Hussars and Cossacks to the outsider is

best indicated by the impressions of a British officer stationed in the Netherlands in 1813: 'They [Russian Cossacks] never sleep in a house, and I saw some at the Hague encamped in a stable yard. Both friends and enemies dislike them, for they take whatever they choose. They swear that on their entry into France they will destroy man, woman and child, and that they will first pillage Paris and then burn it... There are some Bosnian Cossacks, who use bows and arrows, and are quite naked.'[24] Not only is this a pretty typical description of these primitive raiders,

Top left, **Prussian Hussars of the Magdeburg Regiment, c.1800. From their waists hang the** *sabretache,* **literally 'sabrepocket', which was a thin leather case with embroidered flap which served as a writing board and container for military orders, Hussars frequently serving as messengers on the battlefield.**

Above, **Officer of the Prussian Leib Hussars Regiment von Zieten, late 18th century, lithograph by Adolph von Menzel. His remarkable costume of leopard skin cloak, yellow boots, and feathers in his hat show a strong link between the classic Hungarian Hussar costume and that worn by the Polish Winged Hussars.**

but also the 'Bosnian Cossack' is in fact a Hussar in the old sense of the word, for the Serbian word for a bandit is *husar* or *gusar*, the root of the Hungarian *huszar*.

The process by which these freelance maurauders became absorbed into a regular army is similar to that enacted by the English over the Scots Highlanders at the beginning of the 18th century. For a hundred years previously, Hungarian Hussars had fought with the Austrian Habsburg army as maurauding auxiliaries against the Ottoman Turks. Towards the end of the 17th century, the seemingly unstoppable Turkish army had suffered several key reverses. In 1683, a Polish led alliance defeated them outside Vienna. In the years following this, the Austrian Habsburgs piled pressure on the Turks with several campaigns into the Hungarian territory of their empire until they achieved the complete conquest of Hungary and Croatia in 1699 and pushed on into the Balkans where they captured Belgrade in 1718. Having vastly increased the size of their dominions, the Austrians set about consolidating these gains in a similar manner to that of Britain's absorption of Scotland. An element of this union included the formal appearance of Hungarian Hussars in the Austrian army, not merely as auxiliary wild men, but as uniformed, disciplined members of a regular army. Like the Scots Highlanders, the Hussars were allowed to keep elements of their distinctive national costume and this became the basis of the classic Hussar uniform.

By the time of the Seven Years War in 1740, the Austrians had raised several Hussar regiments and they wore the following basic items: a fur hat or busby with a coloured cloth bag hanging from it (derived from the earlier fur trimmed stocking hat); a short fur trimmed coat or pelisse (derived perhaps from the fur lined cloak), often worn like a cape draped over one shoulder; a short jacket or dolman secured with ornamental frogging; tight coloured breeches and Hungarian boots; a sash of coloured cords around the waist; tight breeches and Hungarian boots; an ornamented case or *sabretache* worn from the waist; a decorated saddlecloth or shabraque. The colours of all these varied according to regiment, but could be very bright: Hussars of the Regiment P.A. Esterhazy wore light blue dolmans with yellow cuffs, red breeches, and yellow boots. They fought with their native sabre and carbines (short cavalry muskets). Very quickly they became the most colourful cavalry employed on European battlefields.

Many Western European commanders had served with the Austrians in their campaigns against the Turks and as they returned to their own countries they not only brought attractive reports of these exotic looking figures, but raised their own units modelled after them. The French quickly followed the first regular Austrian regiment raised in 1688 with a regiment of their own in 1692. By the middle of the 18th century, there were seven Hussar regiments in French pay, three of Hungarian origin, four recruited from Germans and Liegois. Even their own French light cavalry, called *Chasseurs à cheval*, were overwhelmed by the Hussar fashion and demanded a similar Hungarian-style uniform. The rakish character of these horsemen, conveying an appeal of illicit, dangerous sex, similar to that surrounding gypsies or pirates, extended even to their hairstyles. French Hussars wore moustaches, a pigtail, and two cadenettes or pleated lengths of hair hanging down each cheek – these being encouraged to hang straight with the aid of hollowed pistol bullets knotted to them. Napoleon later brought an end to this exoticism by ordering Hussars to have their hair cut, although even he could not get them to remove their waxed moustaches. Hussars, however, were not the first East European warriors to serve France as mercenaries. Albanian stradiots and Croatians, all raiding horsemen, had been hired by French armies in the 16th and 17th centuries, the Croats apparently being renowned for wearing scarves around their necks as this is the origin of the word cravat.

The Hussar fashion spread northwards. Several German states raised their own Hussar regiments and during the Seven Years War, Prussian Hussars fought against Hungarian Hussars, the similarity of their uniforms leading to many mistakes, including one incident when an Austrian Hussar trumpeter managed to rally a group of Prussian Hussars around him. The similarity to pirates was enhanced when the Prussian Leib Hussars adopted a skull and

Opposite, flamboyant Napoleonic Hussar painted by Francois Flameng, showing all the swagger and arrogance associated with these soldiers, making them one of the first troop types to actively exploit their sex appeal through their uniform.

Above, Caucasian Cossacks return from a raid on a Turkish settlement in the middle of the 19th century, carrying a captured banner and severed heads tied to their saddles. These bandit warriors retained the original Eurasian style of their Serbian Hussar counterparts long after Hussars had become uniformed regular soldiers. Irregular Cossacks continued to serve the Russian Army in their wild clothes until they were finally given their own uniforms in the late 19th century.

crossbones insignia, or Death's Head, on their hats. Russia added a number of Hungarian-style Hussars to its own army in the Seven Years War, mainly recruited from the Balkans. Being regular troops these cavalry were paid, but they fought alongside groups of Cossacks representing the earlier tradition of raiders dependent on loot and ravaging the enemy to supplement their income. Most of these came from the eastern provinces of the Russian empire, their appearance being more primitive and far less regulated than the Russian Hussars, some even fighting with bows and arrows. It would only be in the 19th century that Russia would finally clothe all its Cossack warriors in a uniform.

Britain largely managed to resist the fashion for Hussar costume throughout the 18th century, despite the presence of the Duke of Cumberland's Hussars at Culloden, and even though regular units of light cavalry or dragoons, dressed similarly to footsoldiers, were informally termed Hussars. During the war against Napoleon, the British employed German Hussars to great effect and finally, in 1807, four regiments of Light Dragoons were converted to Hussars, wearing the full Hungarian-style uniform. Some British publications criticised the overly decorated uniforms, *The Statesman* describing it as 'a mere gee-gaw... subject, by its intrinsic frivolity, to public ridicule'.[25] Proving popular with its wearers, however, Hussar regiments remained in the British Army, winning sterling reputations throughout the 19th century, most notably during the Charge of the Light Brigade at Balaclava. By 1922, there were 12 regiments of Hussars, and today there are two remaining such regiments, The King's Royal Hussars and the Queen's Royal Hussars (The Queen's Own and Royal Irish). A similar Hussar uniform was adopted by the Royal Horse Artillery and this endures today, so that one can see the spectacle of the Queen being saluted on her birthday by guns fired by members of the Royal Artillery wearing the uniforms of Hungarian bandits. The Hussar fashion even crossed the Atlantic to North America where French recruited Hussars of Lauzun's Legion fought in the American War of Independence and a century later Northern volunteers raised their own Hussar units during the American Civil War.

The most spectacular Hussar uniform ever worn must be that belonging to the Polish Winged Hussars of the 16th and 17th centuries. Curiously, the term Hussar seems to be

Colonel Henry Blackburn Hamilton, commander of the 14th (King's) Hussars, 1887-91. His uniform is little different from that worn by Prussian or French Hussars a century earlier, showing the final acceptance of this style by the British Army.

The most exotic of all cavalry uniforms was that worn by the Polish Winged Hussars. This painting by Ron Poulter shows three versions of the wing worn by Polish soldiers. The reconstruction at top shows a Polish Hussar of 1635 wearing the first version of the wing attached to his saddle. The reconstruction at bottom left is based on a portrait of Colonel

Szczodrowski entering Paris in 1645 with an ostrich feather wing mounted on his saddle – his clothes show a strong Turkish influence. The reconstruction at bottom right shows the final form of a Polish Hussar in the early 18th century wearing two wings attached to the back of his armour.

misplaced when describing these warriors, as they are essentially armoured lancers, akin in social status and military performance to French *Gens d'Armes*, gentlemen at arms, but their chosen form of dress owes much to the culture of the border bandit warriors of the Balkans and the Eurasian steppes. In addition to the Turkish-style kaftan and tight breeches, the Polish Hussars wore mail or plate armour, a plumed helmet, a cloak or saddlecloth of leopard or panther skin, and one or two giant wooden wings with ostrich feathers attached to them. In the 16th century, these 'wings' were attached to their saddle, but in the 17th century they were fixed to the back of their armour and gave them perhaps the most elaborate appearance of any warriors at any time.

The origin of the wearing of these wings seems to point back to the feathers worn by hunter-bandits in the Balkans, especially those known as Delis who fought as scouts and raiders for both sides in the wars against Ottoman Turkey, and adorned their helmets, shields, and clothes with the feathers of birds they had killed. Going back further in time, the Huns awarded feathers to their finest archers, two feathers worn in a helmet being a sign of skill at shooting both backwards as well as forwards. The practical purpose of wearing these wings has been investigated and although several theories have been put forward, one being that they made a frightening noise when charging into battle, it seems most likely that they were worn out of sheer extravagance and simply added to an awe-inspiring appearance, like a bearskin cap, which has its own psychological impact on the battlefield. Bernard Connor, an Irishman in Poland in the 17th century, described the appearance of the Hussars as frightful: 'being stuck all over with wings of Storks, Cranes, Turkey-cocks &c. and cloatted over their Armour with skins of Leopards, Tygres, Bears, Lions, etc., all of which they do to make themselves more terrible to the enemy.'[26] This was very much the final development in the most exotic of cavalry types.

17th Lancers (Duke of Cambridge's Own) in 1896. Originally dragoons, they now wear the Polish-inspired Lancer uniform of square-topped *czapska* hat and angled white *kurta* tunic. British cavalry managed to resist foreign cavalry styles until after the end of the Napoleonic Wars when Hussar and Lancer styles were adopted.

GREEN MEN

Hussars were not the only Eastern European wild men to make a world-wide impression through their uniforms. In its wars against the Turks, the Austrian Army also employed irregular footsoldiers recruited from their Balkan border states, such as Croatia. These were called *Grenzers*, and Sir Nicholas Wraxall described them in 1778 as: 'fierce, undisciplined and subject to scarcely any military laws... A degree of primitive rudeness and simplicity characterises them totally unlike the spirit which animates the mercenary stipendiary of modern armies.'[27] They wore Hussar-style jackets with frogging and although their uniforms from the middle of the 18th century comprised many colours, green appeared regularly on jackets and facings.

From their Germanic provinces, the Austrians also raised units of sharpshooters among foresters and huntsmen and these were called *Jägers*. Their uniform usually consisted of a natural undyed grey with green facings, black belts and straps, and sometimes a green feather in their hats. Both *Grenzers* and *Jägers* performed as skirmishers on the battlefield and were frequently armed with the longer-range and more-accurate rifle, rather than the smoothbore musket used by soldiers of the line. When the Prussians confronted these warriors, they were duly impressed and Frederick the Great raised his own *Jäger* battalion in 1786. Another military fashion had been created.

Britain experienced its own savage border war in the American colonies against the French in the middle of the 18th century and one reaction to this was the creation of a unit of Rangers under the command of Richard Rogers. These soldiers acted as Special Forces troops do today, operating deep behind enemy lines, causing mayhem and spreading fear. Originally wearing their civilian hunting shirts of dull, fringed fabric, Rogers' Rangers were later provided with hunting jackets dyed green. By the time of the American War of Independence, the British still appreciated the usefulness of skirmishing riflemen, but in order to show who was in command, green was forgotten and they were clad in regular army scarlet.

Back in Europe, however, the *Jäger* fashion was in full swing and when Britain entered the war against Napoleon, German riflemen were directly hired by the British and they wore a green uniform complete with emblematic hunting horns on their hats. They formed the fifth battalion of the Light Infantry 60th (Royal American) Regiment, and soon afterwards they were joined by a wholly British unit of riflemen called the 95th Foot Regiment. Armed with Baker rifles, the 95th enjoyed an elite reputation as the first and last to fire in a battle. Their uniform was a dark 'rifle' green faced with black and from this time on dark green became the colour of light infantry riflemen and is still worn today by the Royal Green Jackets, an amalgamation of all these earlier units. Paradoxically, although the Germanic *Jägers* frequently wore green facings, the main body of their uniform was actually grey – a shade known as 'pike-grey' composed of 50 per cent natural white wool and 50 per cent blue dyed wool – and this later became the inspiration behind the grey worn by the Confederate Army in the American Civil War.

Rifleman of the 60th King's Royal Rifle Corps in 1845. Nicknamed 'The Green Jackets' and formerly known as the 60th (Royal American) Regiment of Foot, the 5th Battalion was the first regular British infantry unit to be uniformed entirely in green. The hunting horn emblem on his pack and hat refers to the German *Jäger* tradition.

Top, Robert Rogers raised a company of Rangers to serve as scouts and raiders in the French-Indian War of 1754-63. This portrait shows a combination of Indian-style equipment and European clothes typical of that worn by his Rangers, but not the green-coloured hunting shirt said to have been ordered by him as their uniform.

Above, 3rd Goorkhas in the 1880s, painted by Richard Simkin. Their green uniforms demonstrate that they are riflemen to be used in a skirmishing role like all other riflemen in the British Army.

SEX APPEAL

By the end of the 18th century, there was a great shift in the attitude to uniforms. Intended as a mark of servitude and control at the beginning of the century, after a hundred years of successful European campaigning, the army was no longer seen as a gang of freebooters but as something disciplined and controlled which added to the greatness of European civilisation through colonial conquest and national defence. Indeed, it was something to be proud of and those who wore a uniform were due a degree of respect and admiration. In fact, it was more than this, a uniformed man was rather impressive and exciting – he had acquired sex appeal.

Jane Austen captures this mood in her novel of 1813, *Pride and Prejudice*, describing the interests of her younger female characters: 'Their eyes were immediately wandering up in the street in quest of the officers, and nothing less than a very smart bonnet indeed, or a really new muslin in a shop window, could recall them.' And later when a young man is spotted, his one flaw is clearly stated: 'His appearance was greatly in his favour; he had all the best part of beauty, a fine countenance, a good figure, and very pleasing address... the young man wanted only regimentals [a uniform] to make him completely charming.'[28]

The sex appeal of the exotic soldier, such as the Hussar, has already been described, but it was also the ordinary red-coated or blue-coated regular soldier that excited such interest. Some of this was, of course, due to the fact that certain uniforms indicated certain social rank, such as that worn by officers or cavalrymen, but even the ordinary ranker stood a better chance of attracting the ladies in a smart uniform than the average civilian. A uniform spoke of excitement, adventure, manliness, courage and, possibly, wealth. The appeal of the uniform was considered an advantage of joining the army and was exploited by recruiting officers who always wore their smartest uniform before venturing into a pub in search of recruits. The very cut and tailoring of uniforms added to this impression with broad shoulders created by the wearing of 'wings' of braid, short tapered jackets emphasising the waistline, tight breeches showing off legs and buttocks to great effect, and, of course, a tall hat increasing overall height. Even if you possessed the most undesirable body, a uniform could do wonders for you, as described in *The Whole Art of Dress!* of 1830: 'an

Trooper of the 17th Lancers in 1832. His uniform displays many design features created to make military men look good. His gold epaulettes emphasise his shoulders, his short jacket emphasises his chest and long legs, the waistband flattens his belly, his collar keeps his head up and back straight, and his hat increases his overall height.

Caricature of Coldstream Guardsman demonstrating his appeal to women, published in *Army and Navy Drolleries* c.1875.

insignificant head is hidden under a martial plumed helmet. The coat, padded well in every direction... is rendered small at the back by the use of stays... then, as for bandy-legs, or knock-knees, they are totally unseen in long, stiff, leather boots, that extend up on the thigh, to which two inch heels may be very safely appended, so that with the cuirass and different accoutrement straps, it offers an effectual screen.'[29]

Sex appeal was not the only advantage of wearing a uniform in the late 18th century. It was also a matter of political survival. Revolution swept through France in the final decade of the century. The old aristocracy had been overthrown by a group of bourgeois idealists and as the revolution defended itself against threats from inside and outside its borders so it became increasingly militarised, until Napoleon finally took charge and France became a military regime at war with the rest of Europe. In France, it became a matter of political and personal survival to be identified with the revolution and this meant the wearing of a uniform pledging your loyalty to the new regime. Across the Channel, in a Britain terrified that the same chaos might be visited upon them, it became considered fashionable and sensible for the aristocracy to embrace the wearing of uniforms. Not only did this disassociate them from the decadent peacock wear of an ancien regime that was clearly in danger of being swept away, but it also allied the aristocracy with every other member of society who considered it their duty to oppose Napoleon. By donning a scarlet jacket, the British aristocracy transformed the war with revolutionary France from being a class conflict to a conflict of nations in which all members of society stood together against the Napoleonic monster. It was, for Britain, its first world war, its first war in which the whole of society felt a kinship with each other, their backs against the walls against a possible invasion and overturning of their very way of life.

Increasingly, English aristocrats who served in the upper echelons of the army, had themselves painted in portraits not standing in rich clothes beside a classical sculpture, but portrayed in heroic scarlet with a sword attached to their waists and a scene of battle behind them. Between 1750 and 1800, 124 peers and sons of peers served in the various Guards regiments. Over the next half century, this figure almost doubled. And if there was no room in the regular army, then it was considered *de rigueur* to raise your own

militia unit which which to defend the homeland in case of invasion and, of course, much time was devoted to creating a suitably attractive uniform for these privately funded troops.

Despite the advantages of wearing a uniform, however, there has always been a certain quirkiness among the more fashionable elite to buck the trend and this no more so than in the British Army. As early as 1787, a satirical manual entitled *Advice to the Officers of the British Army* recommended the value of standing out from your fellow officer: 'the first article we shall consider is your dress; a taste in which is the most distinguishing mark of a military genius, and the

principal characteristic of a good officer... the fashion of your clothes must depend on that ordered in the corps; that is to say, must be in direct opposition to it; for it would show a deplorable poverty of genius if you had not some ideas of your own in dress... Never wear your uniform in quarters, when you can avoid it. A green or brown coat shows you have other clothes besides your regimentals, and likewise that you have courage to disobey a standing order. If you have not an entire suit, at least mount a pair of black breeches, a round hat, or something unregimental and

Top, **uniform masculinity: officers of 1st Battalion Suffolk Regiment in 1895. Their overall style is impressive, the majority of them wear moustaches and have taken great care with their uniforms. They wear red roses in their caps to commemorate a battle honour won at Minden.**

unmilitary.'[30] Such a posture might be considered playfully anarchic were it not for the fact that at the very summit of the British Army was a man who cared very little for uniforms.

The Duke of Wellington cared little for the detail or fashion of uniform. In a letter of 1811, he writes: 'There is no subject of which I understand so little; and, abstractedly speaking, I think it is indifferent how a soldier is clothed, providing it is in a uniform manner; and that he is forced to keep himself clean and smart, as a soldier ought to be. But there is one thing I deprecate, and that is any imitation of the French, in any manner.'[31] Wellington was referring to the bizarre notion that despite being at war with the French, some administrators, no doubt influenced by an ancien regime passion for anything French, were considering French-style uniforms for the British Army. Already, British Hussars looked like French Hussars and Wellington noted this caused dangerous confusion. He maintained it was important that a British infantryman's hat should look different to a Frenchman's from a distance, and at a distance colour did not so much matter as shape. Despite the glamour it brought to his troops, Wellington was very much against any of the exotic uniforms introduced by special units. He wanted the rifle to be known as a 'rifled musket' or else 'the soldiers will become conceited, and be wanting next to be dressed in green, or some other jack-a-dandy uniform.'

Wellington himself did not wear a uniform, preferring to appear on the battlefield wearing a plain civilian blue coat, buff breeches, and riding boots as though out for a morning canter on his estate, and thus promoting the British character of gifted amateurism. This relaxed attitude was appreciated by his officers. 'Lord Wellington was a most indulgent commander,' recalled William Grattan, 'he never harassed us with reviews, or petty annoyances, which so far from promoting discipline, or doing good in any way, have a contrary effect... Provided we brought our men into the field well appointed, and with sixty rounds of good ammunition each, he never looked to see whether their trousers were black, blue or grey; and as to ourselves (the officers), we might be rigged out in all the colours of the rainbow if we fancied it. The consequence was, that scarcely any two officers were dressed alike! Some with grey braided coats, others with brown; some again liked blue; while many from choice, or perhaps necessity, stuck to the "old red rag".'[32]

Much of this casualness was due also to the fact that on campaign it did not take very long before the parade ground appearance of soldiers disintegrated. This was never more so than during the Peninsular War when British troops went for years without uniform replacements and were reduced to swapping their broken boots for sandals cut out of cowhide. George Wood of the 82nd recalls his appearance: 'Our coats were patched over with different colour cloth... My own coat was mended with the breeches of a dead Frenchman, which I found on the field – the only trophy I yet had to boast of having retained from the spoils of the enemy.' John Patterson of the 50th had an even harder time: 'Our clothes were worn to rags, the jacket being no better than "a thing of shreds and patches", metamorphosed from red to a sort of muddy claret colour; the other garments were... pieced in a manner that would have qualified the wearer to perform the part of Harlequin. The whole attire was surmounted by a nondescript article, vulgarly called a cocked hat, which... formed a good reservoir for rain, its angular point answering the purpose of a waterspout, while the flap hanging over the dorsal region, like that of a London coal heaver, imparted to the owner, a look of a most dubious character.'[33]

Despite the wear and tear of campaign, when it came to entertaining the ladies, officers and men would do their best to improve their appearance. Wellington encouraged the giving of dances and balls whenever his army halted at a Spanish town. The following morning, heads fuzzy with pleasure, officers would mount their horses 'still dressed in their ball attire, such as crimson, light blue, or white trousers, richly embroidered with gold or silver, velvet and silk waistcoats of all colours, decorated in a similar manner; dandies ready alike for the dance and the fight.'[34] So just as the ordinary ranks began to take a pride in their uniform and could see its advantages in attracting women, the more unconventional of the upper ranks took a delight in flouting the rigour of discipline and adopted a more casual approach to uniforms. Mixing it with their own civilian attire, they maintained a nonchalant style which had an aristocratic sex appeal all of its own.

Sergeant-Major Johnstone of the British Cavalry Depot inspects an aspiring cavalryman, c.1896. 'Raw material and the finished article' was the original caption for this photograph, demonstrating the contrast between military and civilian fashions and the appeal for a young man to join the army and get a uniform.

Row 1:

| Infanterist. | Husar. | Kürassier. | Artill.-Offizier. | Infant.-Unteroffiz. | Reit. Artill. | Kürassier. | Artillerist. | Reiter. | Infanterist. | Füsilier-Trommler. | Garde du Corps. | Musketier. | Grenad.-Offiz. | Chevauleger. | Artillerist. Füsilier. Dragoner. Musketier. Grenadier. Kürassier-Offiz. Husar. |

| Oesterreich-Ungarn. 1800. | Kurpfalz-Bayern. 1802. | Württemberg. 1802. | Baden. 1802. | Kursachsen. 1806. | Preussen. 1806. |

Row 2:

| Linien-Infant. | Leichte Infanterie. | Kürassier. | Jäger z. Pf. | Husar. | Artillerist. | Offiz. d. Garde-Grenad. | Ehrengarde. | Linien-Inf. | Leichte Infant. | Kürassier. 1809. | Linien-Inf. | Linien-Inf. 1812. | Garde du Corps. | Garde-Husar. 1812. | Linien-Inf. | Inf.-Offiz. 1812. | Lancier. | Grenadier. Dragoner. |

| Frankreich. 1808. | Italien unter Eugen Napoleon. 1808. | Holland unter Louis Napoleon. | Westfalen unt. Jérôme Napol. | Neapel unt. Joachim Napoleon. | Spanien unter Joseph Napol. | Dänemark. 1812 |

Row 3:

| Inf.-Offizier. | Infanterist. | Kürassier. | Kosak. | Husar. | Musketier. | Landwehr. | Jäger. | Artill. Infanterist. Ulan. Chevauleger. | Leibgarde-Jäger. | Guerilla. | Linien-Infant. | Reit. Artill. | Linien-Infanterist. | Dragoner. | Leichter Dragoner. | Grenadier. | Linien-Infant. | Husaren-Offizier. |

| Russland. 1812. | Preussen. 1813. | Oesterreich-Ungarn. 1813. | Schweden 1813. | Spanien (Nationalheer). 1813. | England. 1815. | Nassau. 1815. | Niederl. 1815. | Braunschw. 1815 |

Military uniforms of Europe 1800 to 1815, painted by Richard Knotel.

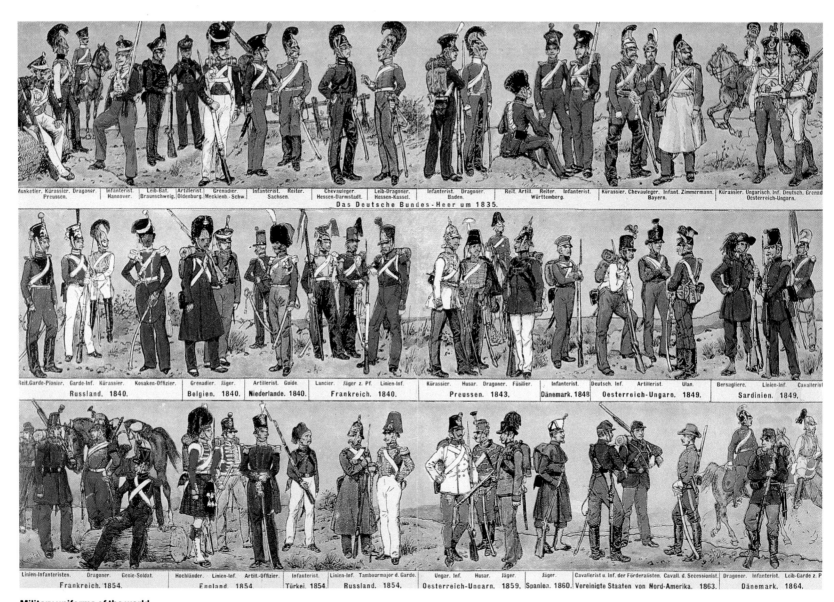

Military uniforms of the world
1835 to 1864, painted by Richard
Knotel.

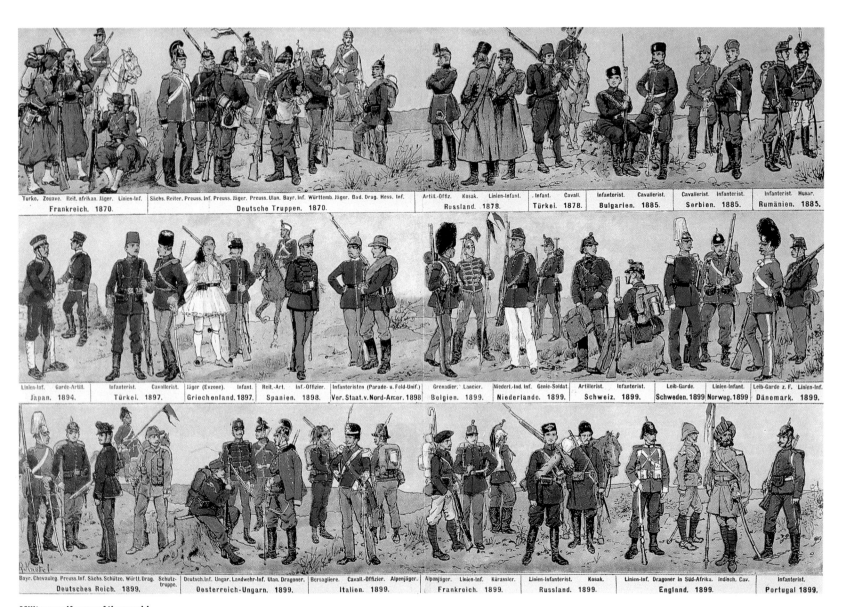

Turko.	Zouave.	Reit. afrikan. Jäger.	Linien-Inf.	Sächs. Reiter. Preuss. Inf. Preuss. Jäger. Preuss. Ulan. Bayr. Inf. Württemb. Jäger. Bad. Drag. Hess. Inf.	Artill.-Offiz.	Kosak.	Linien-Infant.	Infant.	Cavall.	Infanterist.	Cavallerist.	Cavallerist.	Infanterist.	Infanterist.	Husar.
Frankreich. 1870.				**Deutsche Truppen. 1870.**	**Russland. 1878.**			**Türkei. 1878.**		**Bulgarien. 1885.**		**Serbien. 1885.**		**Rumänien. 1885.**	

Linien-Inf.	Garde-Artill.	Infanterist.	Cavallerist.	Jäger (Evzone).	Infant.	Reit.-Art.	Inf.-Offizier.	Infanteristen (Parade- u. Feld-Unif.)	Grenadier.	Lancier.	Niederl.-Ind. Inf.	Genie-Soldat.	Artillerist.	Infanterist.	Leib-Garde.	Linien-Infant.	Leib-Garde z. F.	Linien-Inf.
Japan. 1894.		**Türkei. 1897.**		**Griechenland. 1897.**		**Spanien. 1898.**		**Ver. Staat. v. Nord-Amer. 1898**	**Belgien. 1899.**		**Niederlande. 1899.**		**Schweiz. 1899.**		**Schweden. 1899**	**Norweg. 1899**	**Dänemark. 1899.**	

Bayr. Chevauleg. Preuss. Inf. Sächs. Schütze. Württ. Drag. Schutztruppe.	Deutsch.Inf. Ungar. Landwehr-Inf. Ulan. Dragoner.	Bersagliere.	Cavall.-Offizier.	Alpenjäger.	Alpenjäger.	Linien-Inf.	Kürassier.	Linien-Infanterist.	Kosak.	Linien-Inf. Dragoner in Süd-Afrika.	Indisch. Cav.	Infanterist.
Deutsches Reich. 1899.	**Oesterreich-Ungarn. 1899.**	**Italien. 1899.**			**Frankreich. 1899.**			**Russland. 1899.**		**England. 1899.**		**Portugal 1899.**

**Military uniforms of the world
1870 to 1899, painted by Richard
Knotel.**

AMERICAN BLUE

The political symbolism of colours has had a curious rever-
sal over the last 300 years. For most of the 20th century,
blue has been the colour of conservatism, of government,
whereas red has been the colour of revolution, of opposition. Towards the end of the century, this orthodoxy has
been challenged by blue-swathed Republicans or
Conservatives who have been the true revolutionaries in
economics and government and it is the old-fashioned red
of socialism, as exemplified by the Soviet Union, that has
been overthrown by new ideas. Red as the colour of radical
politics began in the middle of the 19th century when the
nationalist revolutionary Giuseppe Garibaldi clad his Italian
army of followers in red shirts and this was later taken up by
Marxists who adopted a red flag as their sign of the international battle against capitalism. In the 18th century, this
coloured view of politics was very different. Red was the
colour of tyranny and blue was the colour of revolution.

In 1774, representatives of 12 British colonial states in
North America gathered at the First Continental Congress
to co-ordinate their opposition to British rule. A year later,
the supporters of this embryo United States of America
were at war with the British and their fight for independence
had begun. These early revolutionary soldiers were little
more than citizens in arms and they wore a variety of hastily
gathered clothes and equipment. As the war continued, the
army of the United States evolved into a professional force
able to contain and ultimately defeat the British Army. A
century earlier, in the English Civil War, itself a revolution
against monarchy, both sides had not considered different
colour uniforms important enough to invest in, using only
improvised badges of identity, but in North America in the
1770s, political symbolism was accorded more importance
and a general increase of wealth in these mercantile
colonies as well as the growth of a uniforms industry in
Europe meant it was possible for the leaders of this newly
created alliance of states to order complete uniforms for
their rebel troops. The colour they chose was blue. Blue, as
indicated earlier, was the only other cheap dye, after red,
needing just one dyeing stage. It was also the same colour
as that chosen for the background of the white stars in the
famous stars and stripes adopted by the American rebels
as their flag. Finally, it was not the colour of the British Army
redcoats.

George Washington in 1754, wearing the uniform of Colonel of the Virginia Militia, painted by Charles Willson Peale. This blue jacket with red facings would become the basis of the primary U.S. military uniform worn during the War of Independence.

In 1754, however, Washington was serving the cause of the British Empire during the French-Indian War. Around his neck he wears a gorget, an emblem of command in the British Army.

Some 30 years later, a portrait of George Washington as commander of the American Continental army fighting Britain, wearing a blue coat with buff facings, painted by Charles Willson Peale.

By June 1779, an estimate was presented by the Board of War to the Continental Congress for just over 100,000 standardised uniforms consisting of a dark blue jacket, with different colour facings for different units of the army, tin or brass buttons stamped USA, black cocked hats, white waistcoats and breeches. A later General Order of October 1779 instructed the individual states to supply clothing for the army and this was to be of an agreed dark blue base with different colour facings representing different groupings of states. General Washington approved the order, the need for conformity being demonstrated by a delivery received in the same year by the Deputy Clothier General in Philadelphia which included jackets coloured blue, brown, green, black and light blue.

The majority of American revolutionary uniforms were procured from France, with some coming from Spain, one of Benjamin Franklin's duties in Paris being to oversee the purchase of uniforms from the French. Sometimes, this stock of clothing came from unorthodox sources, such as a consignment of British uniforms captured by a Spanish fleet which was passed on to the U.S. agent in Cadiz who shipped it to America where Washington ordered that the redcoats be dyed brown and issued to his soldiers. Such luck cut both ways, however, and American shipments of uniforms were intercepted by the British fleet. The largest single overseas procurement was made in 1777 in France, when 32,000 French-style uniforms were purchased and issued to the Continental Army between 1778 and 1780. A surviving contract for part of this order records 'Ten thousand uniforms, one half of Royal blue cloth and the other half of brown cloth fully lined, with facings and lapels of red, white buttons, waistcoats and breeches of white, twilled Tricot...'.[35] That blue was considered the more popular of the two uniforms is confirmed in an order from Washington who declared that 'to prevent disputes & jealousy among the Troops of the Main Army', as some 'Troops may prefer them (blue) to Brown', a lottery was conducted in which the winning units chose their colour of preference.[36] In Britain too, blue had become recognised as the primary colour of the rebels and in the Houses of Parliament, members of the opposition wore blue coats to provoke the King and his supporters. As the war dragged on into the 1780s, however, American credit abroad slumped and new uniforms became harder to purchase. With blue uniforms being edged out by brown and other practical substitutes such as undyed white, General Washington tried to maintain uniformity through insisting on the use of scarlet facings as well as issuing orders instructing that old jackets be turned inside out and worn again.

In 1783, at the end of their fight for independence, the Continental Congress disbanded the army that had won their freedom. Fearful of any tyranny backed by an armed force, they would trust instead to the militia of each state to protect its citizens at time of war. Only a tiny regular army of some 7,000 men would remain in the form of the First American Regiment. Such an act of trust in its citizen soldiers was rudely disappointed when a small army of mainly militiamen was devastated by an Indian warband in Ohio. A second regular regiment was raised alongside the militia, but in a second confrontation the militiamen failed again and 630 were killed. The need for a substantial regular army was clear and over the next few years it grew in size until in 1812, when Congress declared war on Britain, it numbered 25 regular infantry regiments, but despite the increase in size it was woefully prepared for war and suffered badly in the opening conflicts. Dark blue jackets with red facings and white trousers remained the first uniform of choice for the regular army, particularly as Britain's redcoats were again the enemy, although the general design was based on the British uniform with a stovepipe shako being worn. Later the red facings were changed for blue.

Newly recruited troops in the War of 1812 had to make do with a variety of uniforms, including white summer uniforms meant for wear in the southern states. Black, grey, and brown jackets all appeared as state governments competed with the central government for scarce materials, Britain having set up an effective naval blockade. Captured British uniforms found themselves employed by the Americans who did not dye them but gave them to their military musicians who traditionally wore a uniform the reverse of the main troops. Regular troops clad in grey were first resentful of this make-do uniform, considering it a cloth worn by labourers or slaves, and when they confronted the British they were regarded as militiamen. But at the battle of Chippewa in 1814, grey-clad regulars advanced boldy under heavy fire to gain a famous victory and ever after, the grey uniforms were worn with pride, some sources even suggesting that this resulted in it being adopted as the uniform of the U.S. Military Academy at

West Point. With grey subsequently enjoying a fashion among volunteer regiments, it may be one of the reasons why grey was then adopted by the Confederate forces in the American Civil War.

At the end of the war with Britain, Congress again cut the size of the regular army, but the United States had now reached a point when foreign armies would no longer threaten its integrity and they could concentrate on expanding their own frontiers westwards and southwards. The U.S. Army as an instrument of conquest was born and with it came a greater sense of professionalism and military innovation. When war broke out in 1846 between the U.S. and Mexico, the contrast between the two armies was indicative of a new trend in military dress. The regular Mexican Army wore elaborate and colourful uniforms in the style of Napoleon's soldiers of 40 years earlier, including cavalry fighting with lances, wearing cuirasses and Hussar outfits. The regular U.S. Army wore a simpler, more practical uniform, distinguishing between a dress uniform for parade, and summer and winter fatigue uniforms worn on

Grey-coated U.S. troops advance to victory against the British at the battle of Chippewa in 1814, painted by H. Charles McBarron. At first resentful of having to wear this make-do uniform – the sign of volunteers or even servants – this victory made grey fashionable as a military colour, second only to blue for the American soldier.

campaign. The standard infantry winter fatigue uniform consisted of a short blue shell jacket with white facings (sometimes the jacket had two useful exterior pockets), blue trousers, and a blue forage cap with leather peak and cloth neck flap. The shade of blue was lighter than previous uniforms, being termed sky blue, although in reality it looks a darker grey blue than what we might call sky blue today. The dress uniform coat was dark blue with tails. Officers sometimes wore their dress uniform or a simple long frock coat. The infantry summer fatigue uniform consisted of white cotton jacket and trousers, but these were not worn in Mexico due to the bitter cold of desert nights. Cavalry uniforms were as simple as the infantry ones, being mainly for regiments of Dragoons, who fought as mounted riflemen, although they were considered an elite and originally issued finer quality material jackets of dark blue. Like the infantry they wore a simple, practical forage cap with perhaps the addition of an orange or yellow cap band. This was the official issue, but life on campaign was somewhat different.

The presence of tens of thousands of volunteer troops for the Mexican War put tremendous pressure on the U.S. Quartermaster Department to cope and although most volunteers were eventually clothed in a standard uniform, they also brought with them a more relaxed approach to campaign dress, as the comments of Lieutenant Dana indicate in a letter to his wife: 'We wear all kinds of uniforms here, each one to his taste, some shirtsleeves, some white, some blue, some fancy jackets and all colours of cottonelle pants, some straw and some Quaker hats, and that is just the way, too, that our fellows went into battle.'[37] That officers took this too far by decorating their plain uniforms with gold and silver lace is recorded by Inspector General Hitchcock: 'Some latitude has been rendered necessary from the absence of proper materials in this country (Mexico), particularly in the colors of cloth, but this affords no excuse for officers, not entitled to them, wearing gold and silver lace on their pantaloons and there is no reason why the prescribed shoulder insignia of rank should be departed from. The evil in this latter case has found its way to non-commissioned officers & particularly to hospital stewards some of whom are wearing lace upon their shoulders & adopting fancy dress of all kinds.'[38] A natural desire for flamboyance among the cavalry seems also to have resulted in a considerable alteration to their plain issue.

Captain William Chapman and comrade in the 5th U.S. Infantry during the Mexican-American War of 1846-48.
This early photograph shows the reality of life on campaign, both soldiers dressed in completely non-regulation clothes according to their personal taste.

U.S. Dragoon and Infantry officer in campaign dress during the Mexican-American War of 1846-48, painted by H. Charles McBarron. The fatigue cap and short shell jacket worn by the dragoon are early steps towards a more practical uniform for the U.S. soldier.

Trooper Chamberlain of the 1st Dragoons describes his regiment wearing 'bright red flannel shirts, and black broad brimmed felt hats; this, with their white belts, burnished arms, gay banners and dashing horsewomen galloping up and down our flanks made an effect seldom witnessed in the dull routine of Uncle Sam's service.'[39]

In the American Civil War, we see the culmination of the two uniform traditions of the U.S. Army, the blue and the grey, although the distinction between the two colours and the two armies was not always so clear, particularly at the beginning of the war. Some Northerners went into battle wearing grey and some Southerners wore blue, with the resulting confusion causing deaths and chaos. New York regiments were particularly keen on wearing grey and the 47th New York, or 'Washington Greys', went into battle wearing a red, white, and blue arm-band to distinguish them from the enemy. On the other side, at the battle of First Manassas, the 5th Virginia Infantry were clad in the U.S. regulation dark blue frock coat and 'Hardee' hats, their only concession to uniformity with their comrades being to remove the black ostrich feather worn in their hats as they believed the 'Yankees' would be wearing this. On the whole, however, and certainly as the war progressed, blue was the colour of the North and grey the colour of the South.

For the regular U.S. army which formed the core of the Northern force, dark blue had been prescribed in 1861 as the regulation colour for their jackets, while the trousers remained sky blue (having briefly been dark blue from 1858 to 1861). The dress coat of the Union (Northern) Army was the long frock coat, but the coat worn by the majority of infantry on campaign was the simple sack coat, a short unstructured jacket with no waist, a turnover collar, secured with just four large buttons. They had no braid or decoration, just one inside pocket, and were popular with soldiers for their comfort and popular with the government who found them extremely cheap to make, costing only two dollars each as opposed to the more than six dollars spent on a frock coat. With this sack coat was born a philosophy of simplicity and practicality which continued to guide the U.S. Army into the 20th century.

Ever ready to look at new products, the U.S. Army issued a waterproof blanket that could double as a poncho made out of recently invented vulcanised rubber. The forage cap remained the official and favourite headgear of the U.S.

Union soldier of 31st Pennsylvania Infantry with his family in Camp Slocum, near Washington DC, in 1862, photographed by Mathew Brady. The soldier is comfortably dressed in soft forage cap and short shell jacket, the most popular items of uniform worn by soldiers of both sides during the Civil War.

New York State militiaman in grey uniform, photographed by Mathew Brady. The use of grey early in the American Civil War by Northern volunteer units was confusing and could lead to fatal mistakes. His kit is fully displayed, including a haversack for carrying food and his metal water canteen.

Private Francis E. Brownell of the 11th New York Infantry, 'Fire Zouaves'. His Arab-style uniform is typical of the Zouave style that came from the French Army and was adopted widely by volunteer units in both the North and South during the Civil War

Army on campaign, being protected against rain with the issue of a black oil cloth cover, although some soldiers cut covers out of their gum blankets. As in the Mexican War, this might be the official view, but on campaign a whole variety of adaptions were made to this standard uniform in line with personal tastes and requirements. On top of this there were the myriad volunteer regiments who made up the majority of the Northern Army. Many of these were raised by individual states or groups of citizens, sometimes ethnically based, who wished to furnish their troops in a uniform of their own design. Out of this desire for independence grew the most famous fashion of the Civil War, that of the Zouaves (see the chapter *Westernisation* for a more thorough description), who wore a flamboyant uniform based on that of North African tribesmen, comprising baggy red trousers with embroidered oriental jackets. Other curious uniforms worn by volunteer regiments included the 18th century American Revolution uniforms worn by the Putnam Phalanx (including tricorne hats), bearkskin busbies worn by the Boston Light Infantry, tartan kilts worn by the 79th New York Volunteers, long blue smocks worn by the Rhode Island Detached Militia, and death's head emblazoned busbies and frogged jackets worn by a U.S. Hussar volunteer unit.

Grey was officially adopted by the Confederate forces in June 1861, the regulations specifying tunics of a medium grey with a blueish cast known as 'cadet gray'. Trousers were full cut sky blue and forage caps grey with a band of branch colour. This design is believed to have been the work of a German artist called Nicola Marschall, who based it on the Austrian *Jäger* uniform. Evolving from irregular units of riflemen in the 18th century, regular *Jäger* regiments entered the Austrian army at the beginning of the 19th century. Their *hechtgrau* or 'pike grey' consisted of a mixture of 50 per cent white natural wool and 50 per cent blue dyed wool, thus giving it a blueish tint. The colour proved to be a useful camouflage, being put to the test by the British Army during the Napoleonic Wars: targets of green and red were placed alongside grey with the result that sharpshooters found it most difficult to hit the grey, perhaps because its light tone was closer to the sky at the horizon whereas the other colours created a dark contrasting shape. Whatever its combat advantages, its process of manufacture also had the advantage of being cheap. Further evidence of Austrian influence on the Confederate

Recreated Southern soldiers on parade demonstrate the variety of colours and materials worn by the Confederate Army, from blue through butternut brown to all tones of grey.

Front and Back of a light Parkins butternut shell jacket. Light brown wool and cotton shell jacket worn by Charles A. Parkins, an Englishman who fought with the 3rd Louisiana Infantry. This is the colour known as butternut.

Detail of Parkins jacket showing the brown wool material flecked with white and light blue cotton. The button bears the Pelican insignia of the state of Louisiana.

uniform is proved by the use of the 'Austrian knot' on each sleeve of the regulation officer jacket. However, as stated earlier, there was already a solid precedent for grey uniforms, worn especially by volunteers, in both the War of Independence and the War of 1812, and so its adoption would not have been viewed as the imposition of a foreign uniform, but part of a native military tradition.

Having settled on grey and a particular tone of grey, the reality of the Confederate Quartermaster's Department issuing uniforms to hundreds of thousands of troops meant that this was soon forgotten in the rush to produce wearable clothes. Throughout the war, Confederate Grey could mean anything from a variety of dark and light greys to a range of blues and browns, such as butternut (made of copperas and walnut shells) and beige, as well as a natural white wool called 'wool plain' which one soldier described as 'white, never having been coloured, with the exception of a small quantity of dirt and a goodly supply of grease – the wool had not been purified by any application of water since it was taken from the back of the sheep.'[40] The use of natural white uniforms was not popular, although the 3rd Louisiana Infantry were said to be a lot happier when it was suggested they wear them on a forthcoming expedition through the Yazoo swamps of Mississippi. On another occasion, Northern troops were said to be terrified and bewildered when surrounded by soldiers in white uniforms.

The basic pattern of Confederate uniforms, including the use of shell jackets and forage caps, was similar to Northern forces. Certainly the Confederacy was at an economic disadvantage against the highly industrialised North, but the idea that this meant the Confederate army was poorly dressed, a horde of soldiers dressed in rags, is a myth. The Confederate Quartermaster's Department continued to issue clothes throughout the war and this centralised effort was matched by the explosion of volunteer units from each of the Southern states provided with uniforms of their own choice by local suppliers eager to help the cause. By the end of the war, North Carolina alone had some 92,000 complete uniforms in store. Some contemporaries even claimed that Confederate troops were better dressed than the Union army. As in the North, there was a myriad of exotic uniforms worn by the various state militias. The Zouave fashion proved popular in the South with the Louisiana Tiger Rifles being one of the gaudiest, wearing blue baggy trousers, red shirts, blue jackets with red trim, a

Top, **Lieutenant-Colonel George A. Custer, commander of the 7th U.S. Cavalry, surrounded by Indian scouts. Taken in the 1870s, this photograph shows Custer in full campaign style, wearing a fringed buckskin hunting jacket rather than regular uniform.**

Above, Custer's Demand, **painted by Charles Schreyvogel, shows Custer negotiating with Kiowa Indian chiefs. His buckskins contrast with the regular uniform worn by the cavalryman behind him, creating an image of frontier freedom and independence still popular today in the United States.**

tasselled red cap and white gaiters over striped socks. In Texas, the 8th Texas cavalry were renowned for taking animal skin clothes to an extreme, with one wearing bearskin trousers and another wearing a full bearskin suit. Texan cavalry Captain Richardson posed for a photograph wearing Jaguar skin trousers with matching Jaguar skin holsters. The ethnic variety of soldiers volunteering from many immigrant communities could be seen in all its richness in Louisiana with units from New Orleans including the Legion Française (wearing French blue infantry dress), the Garibaldi Legion (wearing grey trousers, red jacket and black cocked hat with black plume), the British Guard (a uniform of white faced with blue and silver), and the Belgian Guard (dark green frock coats trimmed with yellow).

The American Civil War was the last major war in which the colour of uniforms really seemed to matter, the Blue and the Grey embodying each side's cause. Colourful uniforms would continue to be worn, increasingly on parade, still into battle, but the days of the bright, display uniform were numbered. The age of machines had engulfed warfare and soon all would be swept away by a tide of khaki. Already in the U.S. Army a good deal of practical design had replaced the more ostentatious uniform ideas of the Napoleonic era and this continued as the U.S. Army reduced in size after the Civil War and returned to its purpose of patrolling and maintaining its mighty territory of states. The U.S. Cavalry was an important instrument in this occupation and it is here that we see the continued pursuit of practicality in military uniforms. Broad-brimmed hats and neckerchiefs were useful in the hot, dusty regions of New Mexico or the Great Plains. Bandoliers were introduced to hold cartridges in little leather loops attached to a shoulder belt, thus giving quick access to ammunition in an ambush. In the wilderness, non-regulation items featured strongly, with soldiers buying their own shirts, boots and hats according to comfort and taste, the most famous of these being the buckskin fringed hunting jacket worn by George Custer, commander of the 7th Cavalry. Custer's death in 1876 at the battle of the Little Bighorn, in which a Sioux and Cheyenne war party wiped out a cavalry patrol, raised the idiosyncratic commander into a frontier icon and his personalised uniform epitomised the spirit of Western man on the edge of civilisation battling against savagery, a combination of individual freedom and going native.

Such was the impact of this frontier image on East Coast sensibilities that when it was captured in oils by the painter Charles Schreyvogel it caused a scandal in civilised circles. Shreyvogel's painting, *Custer's Demand*, depicting the cavalry commander negotiating with Kiowa Indian Chiefs, was criticised by the renowned Western artist Frederic Remington for its lack of authenticity. He quoted uniform regulations of the period, saying Custer and his soldiers would not have looked as they did in the painting, but Custer's widow came to Shreyvogel's defence and gave an indication of life out West. 'Though the regulations were so strict as to uniform in garrison,' she wrote, 'on a campaign great freedom was allowed. The red necktie, buckskins and wide felt hat were the unvarying outfit of my husband on a campaign, while the troops' boots were those made by the Philadelphia bootmaker who shod so many distinguished feet in our service. This freedom with regard to costume and equipment adds much to the picturesqueness of the column on the march.'[41] A veteran of the Indian wars added his own observations to the debate, declaring that Custer did not wear the boots depicted in the painting but actually preferred wearing Indian moccasins in hot and dry weather. 'Of course it must be very annoying to a conscientious artist,' concluded the old soldier, 'that we were not dressed as we should have been, but in those days our uniforms were not according to regulations and were of the "catch as catch can" order.'[42] Practicality was now the dominant theme in military uniforms towards the end of the 19th century, the process having been set in motion in Europe by the demands of their own frontier wars fought all around the globe in the name of Empire.

Lieutenant S.C. Robertson, U.S. Cavalry Chief of Crow Scouts, painted by Frederic Remington in 1890, demonstrating the more campaign ready uniform, including broad-brimmed hat and leather trousers, worn in the U.S. Army towards the end of the 19th century.

Khaki uniforms worn by the U.S. Army during the Spanish-American War of 1898 and afterwards, painted by Henry Alexander Ogden. The culmination of a century's progress towards more practical uniforms, they also show the influence of British colonial wear in the form of sun helmets.

BIRTH OF THE PRACTICAL

The battle of Waterloo and the defeat of Napoleon brought no rest to the armies of Europe. Imperial adventures commanded the attention of all major powers, especially Britain, the greatest of them all, who sent its soldiers to all corners of the world. The demands of these global campaigns was particularly tough on the ordinary soldier who was expected to cope with all terrains and climates despite wearing a uniform that was primarily designed for fighting in Western Europe. Wearing the same set of clothes he might wear on parade outside Buckingham Palace, a British soldier could find himself knee-deep in a paddy field in Burma or shivering behind a snow-covered palisade in Canada. As in Spain, during the Peninsular War, local alterations and conversions were made to the standard uniform, but this was not official and was not allowed for by the regulations set by the military headquarters at Horse Guards in London.

Criticism of the impracticality of military uniforms came most strongly from soldiers themselves. Colonel John Mitchell in his *Thoughts on Tactics and Military Organisation* in 1838 concluded: 'We can promise the best thanks of the soldiers to the first authority that shall rid the service of the bear-skin caps, infantry and light cavalry chakos, the ill-shaped helmet of the dragoons, the jack-boots, cuirasses, and leather-breeches of the life-guards, the stiff leather stocks of the whole army... Why a soldier's dress should be as much as possible calculated to cramp his exertions...we leave to the ingenious to discover.'[43] But it was the question of money that made real inroads into the extravagances of uniform established in the 18th century. In 1843, the Board of General Officers proposed a reduction in the quantity and quality of lace and other decoration worn by the 11th Hussars, thus saving an annual expenditure of £400. Unsurprisingly, these cuts were carried out under the Duke of Wellington who had been appointed Commander-in-Chief in 1842 and continued to sanction reductions in expenditure.

The relaxed attitude of officers on service abroad also contributed to a mood of reform. In tropical climates, maximum use was made of undress clothing, that is, the clothing worn by soldiers when at rest and for all other tasks other than fighting. The shell jacket made its appearance, a simple, single-breasted jacket without lapels or tails. To this

The reality of British soldiers on campaign in South Africa, their trousers torn to shreds. A lack of replacement uniforms meant that most British soldiers on campaign patched their clothes with anything to hand, including sacking and bags containing food.

Opposite, Boer soldiers photographed c.1900. Wearing their own farming clothes, these irregular soldiers caused great havoc among the British Army in South Africa with their guerrilla tactics, hastening the final adoption of practical uniform measures such as the wearing of khaki for the entire army.

was added the soft-topped forage cap, peaked for officers, unpeaked for other ranks. In colder climates, the blue frock coat, a civilian item, became popular among officers to the extent that the *Naval and Military Gazette* reported in 1845: 'The blue frock has become almost the real uniform of the officer; that in which he works and performs his duties on parade and in the field.'[44] By 1848, however, the frock coat was perceived to encourage 'slovenly habits' and was banned in favour of the shell jacket as the universal undress item. In 1852, popular pressure saw the re-introduction of the frock coat but only for 'when riding or walking in the neighbourhood of their Quarters'.[45] For the ordinary soldier, the smock frock made its appearance. Designed originally as an item to wear over a uniform to protect it while on board a ship on a long voyage, it continued to be worn when soldiers arrived in a hot land. Being both light in weight and dyed a deep brown, an early form of camouflage, they proved highly popular. Indeed, the diary entry of Sir Charles Pasley in 1852 in South Africa reveals the extent to which undress and civilian fashion predominated: 'The Officers all wear plan (plain) clothes – the men smock frocks, the former shooting jackets.'[46]

This desire for a looser, simple coat that was both easy to wear and yet long enough to wrap around the waist and upper legs culminated in the 1855 reforms to military uniform in the British Army. A report in the *United Services Magazine* of 1843 makes clear the thinking behind it: 'It has generally been allowed by medical men that bowel complaints, dysenteries, and other diseases, to which the soldier is through exposure liable, may greatly be obviated by keeping the lower parts of the body dry and warm. For this purpose flannel belts were some years ago introduced into the British Army, and nearly the same object is accomplished by the new "build" of the Prussian infantry coat, which is a blue frock, with scarlet facings, reaching to the knees, and lapping over the belly and thighs.'[47] Thus, as a result of practical experimentation in both the British and other nations' armies, the official British battledress of the tight fitting coatee with tails, so typical of the Napoleonic Wars, was finally replaced in 1855 with a tunic with full skirts all round. For officers, the expensive and elaborate gold epaulettes and braid wings were abandoned in favour of rank badges worn on either side of the collar. A lighter tunic was allowed for in India. The height of the tall shako hat was reduced. But reform did not stop here. Campaigning

abroad continued to set the pace for new ideas.

The severe cold of the Crimean War in southern Russia saw British soldiers wearing sheepskin coats and fur hats. A wool jacket, or 'cardigan', buttoning at the front, gained its name from the Earl of Cardigan who led the notorious Charge of the Light Brigade during this war, as did the 'balaclava', a knitted woollen hood covering the whole head named after the battle in which the charge took place. In India, the greatest change of all to the future of uniforms was initiated when troops began to dye their undress uniforms a muddy colour called 'khaki'. 'Puttees' were copied from the Indian practice of wrapping cloth bandages around the lower legs to provide protection and support above the boots. Sun helmets of canvas stretched over a light wicker frame with a crested air vent were popular among civilians and were bought privately by officers who sometimes equipped entire units with them as protection against the sun became necessary; an additional cloth, a puggaree, was generally wound round them to the keep them cool. Forage caps remained popular with ordinary soldiers, being replaced by the Glengarry peakless cap, finally giving way in the 1860s to the sun helmet with air

Sergeant Seymour of 2nd Gordon Highlanders photographed as a mounted infantryman in 1896. His uniform demonstrates the fruits of practical experience in campaigning, including puttees wrapped around the lower legs, riding breeches, short comfortable jacket and a bandolier for carrying ammunition.

Major-General J.M. Babington, commander of the First Cavalry Brigade in South Africa during the Boer War of 1899-1902. Despite the practical mail epaulettes on the shoulder of his jacket, this soldier displays the great pleasure and pride to be derived from wearing a dress uniform.

vent as it became the official item of tropical headwear. In 1877, the sun helmet was refined by replacing the air vent crest with simple ventilation holes around the crown; it was made of cork, coloured white and then later stained light brown.

A quilted neck cover was sometimes added in areas of extreme sun. A final addition in the direction of late 19th century uniform fashion was the addition of a spike on top of the sun helmet in the German style.

The practical reform of uniforms was matched by an improvement in the equipment carried by soldiers. In the 17th and early 18th centuries, a soldier's personal possessions and his food were kept in a cloth snapsack or knapsack which was slung over one shoulder, while other items of equipment and ammunition were first kept in small leather bags attached to a bandolier and later placed in leather boxes attached to another belt slung over the other shoulder. By the end of the 18th century the knapsack had developed into a leather or calfskin pack to which a rolled blanket or greatcoat was strapped and this was attached to the back of the soldier by means of shoulder straps. A separate leather cartridge box, along with a bayonet or

Bullet pierced khaki sun helmet worn by a soldier of the Somerset Light Infantry in the 1880s.

Lieutenant-Colonel G.H.C. Hamilton, commander of the 14th (King's) Hussars during the Boer War, in full khaki campaign dress, including sun helmet and bandolier.

sword, hung at the waist on white leather crossbelts, the crossbelts forming a distinctive part of European uniforms. A wooden or metal canteen or water container hung on another shoulder belt, adding to the load. Each soldier was now expected to be self-sufficient, no baggage wagons would carry his equipment, and the misery of marching with full kit was introduced. In the Peninsular War, French commanders issued their soldiers with up to 15 days worth of bread to add to their self-sufficiency, but Wellington was suspicious of his soldiers who tended to eat as much as they could in one day and then give the rest away, while ammunition was frequently sold for liquor, anything to reduce the weight of the pack, although Wellington countered this with frequent inspections.

In the early 19th century, the back pack was strengthened with a wooden frame but little effort was made to design it for greater comfort. A later military report on load carrying described the effects of this kit, starting with the crossbelts and cartridge box, 'tight over the chest and bumping the man's posterior. The knapsack straps cut the shoulders; and cause swelling, weakness and numbness of the hands and arms lasting up to 24 hours after a march with loss of strength and pressure on the nerves, muscles and blood vessels.'[48] Enough was enough, and by the middle of the 19th century, soldiers on colonial campaigns in hot and difficult climates frequently jettisoned their full packs, carrying only essentials and ammunition. In 1871, the British Army responded by issuing Valise Equipment. The old-style back pack was replaced with a black waterproof canvas bag or valise supported by shoulder straps or braces attached to a waist belt which had two pouches attached to the front of it, each holding twenty rounds of ammunition, as well as a bayonet. With the disappearance of crossbelts, the kit was now better balanced, shifting the burden of weight from the back and shoulders to the waist, but more improvements were to come. In 1882, a new pattern Valise Equipment raised the height of the back pack to ride on the shoulders with the greatcoat rolled beneath it to rest on the waist. An all-purpose tool in the form of a small spade and pick on one handle for digging trenches was added to the waistbelt. A further improvement was made with the Slade-Wallace system, making removal of items easier, but the big breakthrough came with the introduction of webbing, strong woven cotton belts which replaced leather belts and considerably lightened and

Royal Welsh fusiliers c.1900. The private with the regimental mascot wears the Slade-Wallace pattern equipment and straps introduced in 1888, while the pioneer on the left wears the practical clothes of a bygone Napoleonic age in which a military engineer wore an apron and carried an axe.

Opposite, **British Private of the Devonshire Regiment in full Marching Order of the 1890s, painted by Bryan Fosten. He is surrounded by front and back views of his Slade-Wallace valise and pouches, plus canteen and mess tin and marching boots. His cloth-covered spiked helmet follows the German fashion for the** *Pickelhaube.*

improved the flexibility of a soldiers' pack.

Leather bandoliers had become popular in the U.S. Army and were adopted by the British Army during the Boer War, although the loops holding the bullets on these shoulder belts were not the most efficient means of containing ammunition. A Boer soldier during the war in South Africa recalled being able to track British cavalry by the bullets that slipped from their cartridge belts, adding these to his own store of ammunition. The U.S. Army took this development further by adopting woven web bandoliers which were used in their war in the Philippines. An American manufacturer, William Lindsey, brought this innovation to the attention of the British War Office and the result was the opening of a branch of the American Mills Equipment Company in London to produce webbing in all forms of belts and straps, not just as bandoliers. This created a unified system of webbing holding all equipment in which the cross straps were transferred to the back, leaving a soldier's chest unrestricted, and enabling the easy removing of all his equipment in one go, or separately if wished, without upsetting the balance of essentials such as ammunition pouches in front and water bottle behind. The British Army accepted this as the basic infantry equipment in 1908, but because of webbing shortages in 1914, a leather version persisted throughout the war. American soldiers were more complete in their use of webbing and their soft-form webbing equipment and pack may have been one of the reasons for their World War One nickname of 'doughboys' (although a complicated story of U.S. footsoldiers being dubbed 'adobes' because of being covered in dust on a Mexican expedition is another contender). In the late 1930s, webbing finally prevailed in the British Army and a complete system of webbing belts and straps was adopted. The average British and American soldier now had a fully practical, flexible and weight effective method of carrying his equipment.

These were the crucial steps in a long line of progress from display to function, making military clothing practical. No longer was a uniform intended solely as a mark of subservience and control. It was to become a tool of the fighting man, intended to help him carry out his tasks. With this profound change in the philosophy of uniform, we see also the birth of a new uniform aesthetic which would be both utilitarian and modern.

WESTERNISATION

The idea of military uniformity had been understood for
centuries in Asia. In China during the Six Dynasties period
in the 6th century, different armies had worn different
coloured clothes to distinguish themselves. In Ottoman
Turkey in the 15th century, the Janissaries wore different
coloured sashes to denote rank. In the 16th century,
Japanese footsoldiers were supplied with uniform armour,
and in the case of Date Masamune, all his bodyguards wore
tall cone-shape gold-lacquered helmets. In India in the 7th
century, it was noted that not only did *kshatriya* warriors
wear red cloaks and red ornaments, but they also lived in
red houses and stained their teeth red as well.

This use of uniformity was frequently one based on caste
and came from a civilian life where different classes wore
different clothes. In war, warriors would wear their civilian
clothes with armour and be identified additionally by a
colour pertaining to a clan or commander or have a uniform
emblem attached to their garb. Little different in fact from
the uniformity of the ancient world of Greece and Rome or
the heraldic devices of medieval Europe. In contrast, the
18th century European concept of a tailored uniform
designed especially for battle with nation, regiment and
rank indicated in a variety of minute details such as badges,
facings and buttons, appears to be a uniquely Western
invention. Not only is it an expression of a Western interest
in organised detail, but it is also an indication of enormous
material wealth, for few other nations outside of Europe
could afford to bring an army onto a battlefield thus
equipped. As European imperial power spread around the
globe in the 18th and 19th centuries, other cultures began
to copy this Western attribute in an attempt to hopefully
mimic other aspects of Western military success such as
discipline and cohesion.

Mughal India in the 18th century was one of the few other
cultures in the world that could match Europe for material
wealth and it is unsurprising that it should be among the
Indian princes opposing British expansion in this land that
Western-style uniforms should first appear outside of
Europe. Much of the inspiration for this development came
from French soldiers seeking to counter British influence by
giving military advice on tactics and weaponry to Indian
princes. The impact of this was almost immediate. At the

Opposite, Turkish Janissaries on
parade at the end of the 16th
century. Although the Ottoman
Turkish army used different
clothing materials to designate
status and unit and sometimes
elaborate insignia worn on hats,
they did not wear uniforms as
understood in Europe from the
17th century onwards.

**A uniformed infantryman in Tipu
Sultan's Indian army at the end
of the 18th century, watercolour
by Charles Gold. Armed with
muskets, sometimes trained by
French officers, these soldiers
were intended to match the
British forces in discipline and
organisation and the adoption
of a uniform was believed to help
with this.**

Battle of Plassey in 1757, Robert Clive defeated a native army ten times larger, but 50 years later in the war with the Marathas, Major Thorne could comment: 'the changes that have taken place among the warlike tribes of India through the introduction of European tactics and French discipline which, combined with their natural courage often bordering on enthusiastic frenzy, and their numerical superiority, has rendered our conflicts with them sanguinary in the extreme.'[49]

The Hindu Marathas were among the most powerful forces in India, challenging not only British influence but also the Mughal empire. They recruited many Europeans to officer their armies and prince Sindhia went as far as creating battalions of native infantry dressed in red coats, blue turbans and black leather equipment, his cavalry wearing green coats with red turbans. The Nabob Omdat ul Omrah of the Carnatic was even more specific in his borrowings, and clad his bodyguard in the uniform of the British 10th Light Dragoons. Another potent force was that of Mysore, led by Tipu Sultan, and a late 18th century watercolour by Charles Gold portrays one of his soldiers in a blue coat with white crossbands, white breeches, and a red turban. Tipu Sultan supplied many of his troops with the latest weapons, including a unit armed with rockets. Lieutenant Ewan Bushby gives a detailed description of the uniform worn by one of Tipu's 'tiger' soldiers in 1795: 'The dress of the regular infantry is generally of purple woollen stuff, with white diamond formed spots on it, which is called the tyger jacket [this diamond-shaped version of a tigerstripe appeared throughout Tipu's realm as his personal emblem]. On the head is worn a muslin turban, of a red colour, and round the waist a cumberband or sash, of the same. Their legs and feet are entirely naked, excepting a kind of sandal slipper, worn to protect their soles from the roughness of the march.'[50]

As Western powers consolidated their hold on colonies around the world, so they were compelled to employ native warriors alongside their own regular soldiers. In India, native soldiers fighting for the British were called sepoys and were provided with uniforms similar to the British. At first, as with previous waves of conquered foreign troops, the idea of the uniform was to subjugate and discipline them, but as the Indian regiments became an established and valued part of the Imperial army, particularly after the great Indian Mutiny had been suppressed in 1858, so their uniform was relaxed

Infantry of the 15th Sikhs in the British Army of India, 1888, painted by H. Bunnett. They wear a combination of native turban and baggy trousers with the standard scarlet jacket. After the Indian Mutiny of 1857, Indian troops were generally issued with inferior weapons to those carried by British soldiers.

Indian sepoys serving in the army of the East India Company, the main military force of British interests in India in the early 19th century. This watercolour of 1845 by R.D. Moore depicts (left) an officer of Native Cavalry, (middle) havildar or sergeant of 32nd Madras Infantry, and (right) sepoy of 32nd Madras Infantry.

and adapted to their own costume style, with baggier trousers, looser cut tunics, turbans for Sikhs, *kukri* knives for the Gurkhas. However, whereas the 18th century wave of foreign troop styles had become highly fashionable among the rest of the non-foreign army, these Asian styles, perhaps because they belonged to the 'darker' races, did not bridge the gap and remained the badge of native auxiliaries. The one major exception to this was the introduction of khaki, which originated among the native troops of northern India and then swept over the rest of the British Army.

The story was similar in colonial Africa and the West Indies, except that in French North Africa a major style was invented that did capture the imagination of white soldiers in both Europe and America. The Zouaoua tribesmen of North Africa were recruited alongside French settlers and became famous for their bravery and exploits. Later, these Zouave regiments, now composed completely of white Frenchmen, fought in the Crimean War in Russia and won more celebrity, and it was there that U.S. General George B. McClellan saw them and declared they were the 'beau ideal of a soldier'. A precedent for this in the French army was that of Napoleon's Mameluke cavalry, originally recruited from Egyptian warriors but later filled with native Frenchmen who continued to wear oriental clothes. The classic Zouave uniform was Arabic in style and included very baggy trousers, a waist sash, short embroidered jacket and a fez (not dissimilar in fact to that of the Mamelukes). Amazingly, this fancy dress uniform became an instant hit among the many volunteer units that arose in the Northern states at the beginning of the American Civil War. Elmer E. Ellsworth is credited with starting the craze in America. Inspired by the stories told to him by a surgeon in the French Army during the Crimean War, he raised a unit of volunteer New York firemen who called themselves the Fire Zouaves, wore red shirts and baggy blue trousers, and shaved their heads like the original French soldiers. Way out west in Indiana, the Zouave style was modified to a chasseur uniform because the Christian founder of Wallace's Zouaves did not want his soldiers wearing a wholly Muslim outfit.

The most authentically dressed Zouaves were the 5th New York, Duryee's Zouaves, and Alfred Davenport, who served with them, has preserved a complete description of their outfit: 'A more picturesquely unique and fantastical costume could scarcely be conceived. The breeches were wide flowing Zouave pants of a bright red, narrow and

Caricature of Indian Army Horseman in *Army and Navy Drolleries* c.1875. This fierce Sikh warrior is dressed largely in native costume despite being part of the British Army in India and shows the extent to which native clothes were incorporated into the army uniform system.

Recreation of the uniform of a soldier of the 5th New York, Duryee's Zouaves, 1862. This exotic Arab-inspired outfit was one of the rare examples of non-European warriors influencing the style of a Western uniform, volunteer units during the American Civil War being among its most enthusiastic wearers.

Soldiers of the international forces stationed at Tientsin in China in 1911. These photographs demonstrate the extent to which European-style uniforms had been adopted throughout the world as an indication of advanced military power and imperial influence. *This page:* top left, Scottish soldiers in the British Army; top right, Indian soldiers in the British Army; bottom left, Chinese government soldiers; bottom right, Russian soldiers. *Opposite page:* top left, Belgian soldier; top right, Austrian marines; bottom left, French soldiers; bottom near right, Japanese soldiers; bottom far right, German soldiers.

pleated at the top, wide at the bottom and baggy in the rear. These were topped with a broad sash of the same colour edged with blue tape and falling nearly to the knee on the life side. The jacket was of a coarse blue material, trimmed with red tape, short, loose, low-necked and collarless... The caps were close-fitting red fezzes turned back from the top of the head, to which was attached a cord with a blue tassel that dangled down in the middle of the back.'[51]

Despite such eccentric exceptions, the main direction of influence of uniform styles was from Europe to the rest of the world, even when the style did not suit the climate or ethnic nature of the soldiers it was forced upon. The Mexican army, for example, was closely modelled on the Napoleonic army and in the Corps of Sappers (trench-diggers) it was traditional for soldiers to wear full beards, but among its many native American recruits this growth of facial hair was impossible and so the Mexican army ordered them to wear false beards instead. In the Persian army, a compromise was struck between irregular troops clad in mail and traditional costume fighting with bows and swords, alongside regular soldiers with muskets equipped in European jackets with epaulettes and frogging but volumi-nous trousers and conical fur hats. In 1807, an attempt to introduce Western-style uniforms into the Ottoman Turkish army ended in mutiny, the deposition of the Sultan, and the officials responsible for it were torn to pieces in the streets of Constantinople. By 1826, however, a new Sultan was ready for trouble and imposed a dark blue uniform on the Janissaries which they wore until 1909. The trend was unstoppable and even Japan, which had withstood west-ernisation until 1853, transformed its feudal forces in the 1870s into a modern army based on the German model with its Samurai serving as officers and its soldiers wearing a Prussian-style uniform. The fruits of this revolutionary change were soon to be seen when Japan, alone of all the Asian countries, defeated one of the Western Great Powers in the Russo-Japanese war of 1905. The uniform had become universal and with its dispersal some of the appar-ently magical power of the West had slipped into the hands of other equally aggressive cultures.

Contemporary Japanese print depicts the capture of a Russian redoubt by the Japanese Army at Yugaku Chone during the Russo-Japanese War of 1904-05. Uniformed Japanese warriors devastated the Russian Army in the first major war won by a non-European army over a Western Power. Much had been learnt of the Western way of war from studying the Prussian Army and its style influenced Japanese uniforms.

Contemporary Japanese print for an English audience underlines the great revolution in Japanese warfare at the end of the 19th century. The crossing of the Yalu during the Russo-Japanese War by modern uniformed troops is compared with a famous Samurai river-crossing of the 12th century – the fighting spirit is the same, but the military system is radically different.

The 7th King's African rifles c.1955, showing Regimental Sergeant Major Shabari with drummer, bugler and Sambura tribesman, a new recruit to the unit. This photograph depicts a final echo of British Imperial presence in Africa as expressed through its military use of native soldiers.

**Cover of *Armed Europe*
published c.1900 with
illustrations by Richard Simkin.
This popular book of uniforms
was aimed at boys, reflecting a
growing fascination among the
civilian population of the West
for the detail of military
uniforms. It was matched by
other popular pastimes such as
collecting toy soldiers.**

KHAKI

During the 18th century, the majority of Western armies fought as lines of uniformed soldiers letting off a hail of musket-fire at short range and then charging with bayonets fixed. This served very well when the enemy fought in the same style, but in colonial struggles around the world, a new style of guerrilla warfare had evolved in which individual skirmishers armed with rifles ranged across a battlefield, picking off brightly clothed soldiers. This threat did not affect so much nations who wore dark blue or grey uniforms, but it most certainly played heavily on the British in their scarlet jackets.

In North America, isolated attempts were made by specialist units fighting with the British to break away from the vulnerable red. In the middle of the century, Rogers' Rangers adapted traditional hunting shirts into a green uniform and in 1796 the Militia of Upper Canada wore brown coats. In 1835, Light Regiments sent to Canada were to be clothed, according to the *United Services Gazette*, 'in grey – a cloth very much the colour of the bark of a tree. This is a very popular change, as there will be much bush fighting, and our "redcoats" will not be so good an object for the American or Canadian riflemen.'[52]

Colour-Sergeant and Private of the Gloucester Regiment showing the old red jacket and the new khaki uniform c.1900. By 1902, khaki was standard home service dress, making scarlet a purely ceremonial colour in the British Army.

Clearly, the idea of camouflage was very well appreciated by the ordinary soldier, and this improvised development took a further step in 1846 in India. There, a British officer called Harry Lumsden raised a combination of native infantry and cavalry in the Punjab and his Corps of Guides was the first unit of the British Army to wear a loose fitting uniform of 'khaki', or 'drab', as it was then known. Khaki is an Urdu word meaning dusty or dust-coloured, coming from the Persian word for dust, *khak*. Drab is an English word perhaps derived from the Dutch *drab* meaning dregs. Inspired by the demands of fighting in the dusty frontier land of northern India, this first recorded use of khaki is best described as a muddy colour, more grey than brown or green. At a conflict in Sangao in Yusufzai county in 1849, a British gunner stopped his own men firing on the khaki-clad soldiers by shouting out to an officer: 'Lord! sir; them is our mudlarks!'[53] By 1851, a majority of native infantry in the Punjab Irregular Force were wearing khaki uniforms of smock shirts and loose 'pyjama' trousers. For the regular British army, however, it would take more than just a good idea to remove them from their scarlet tunics.

In 1857, British rule in India was shaken by an uprising of native troops. The subsequent, bitter campaign of suppression was fought at the height of the Indian summer in temperatures of 90 degrees Fahrenheit and upwards. The fierce heat and the urgency of the fighting meant that strict rules on uniform were relaxed and many British regiments fought in their undress uniforms of light white jackets and trousers. Quickly dirtied on campaign, these soldiers sought some kind of uniformity by adopting the 'khaki' of their native allies; dyeing their uniforms with anything to hand, including tea, earth, curry powder, and the juice of berries. The resulting array of muddy colours, ranging from grey to brown, was also termed khaki. With no standard colouring, it was sometimes difficult for civilians to distinguish these British soldiers from the natives and one Englishwoman, on viewing the khaki-clad 75th at Agra, declared 'those dreadful-looking men must be Afghans'.

The practicality of this development was officially recognised in the British Army by the Adjutant-General on May 21st, 1858: 'With the concurrence of the government, the Commander-in-Chief is pleased to direct that white clothing shall be discontinued in the European regiments of the Honourable Company's Army; that for the future the summer clothing of the European soldiers shall consist of two suits of "khakee" corresponding in pattern and material with the clothing recently sanctioned for the Royal Army of England.'[54] Here then was an attempt to introduce some standardisation into the use of khaki, but that official army policy-makers were unhappy with its improvised nature was demonstrated when this order was countermanded immediately after the war and khaki disappeared from regular service dress for another 20 years. A decision not altogether unwelcome among the ordinary ranks, for many considered the khaki uniform a poor replacement for their smart scarlet jackets and rather than be seen in public in this 'scruffy' outfit, stayed in their barracks with a resulting rise in drunkenness.

Despite cutting short the khaki experiment, the idea of more sensibly clad soldiers fighting colonial wars in non-regulation uniforms grew apace. In New Zealand, British soldiers were faced with gun-armed Maori warriors and when storming one of their forts, the *Illustrated London News* of 29 August 1863 declared the British soldiers were 'not dressed in red. Every man wore a forage cap and blue frock [coat] the better to conceal him from the sharp eyes of

The Corps of Guides painted by Richard Simkin in the 1880s. A combination of infantry and cavalry raised in northern India by Harry Lumsden in 1846, this was the first unit in the British Army to wear khaki uniforms.

the enemy.'⁵⁵ In 1873, a grey-brown tweed jacket was designed especially for fighting in West Africa during the Ashanti War and, in 1879, against the Zulus, white helmets and belts were stained with tea. Eventually, the British Army had to accept the inevitable and in 1885, a khaki of a brown hue was introduced as standard service dress in the Indian Army and this became universal for all foreign service outside Europe in 1896. Finally, following the traumatic war in South Africa against the rifle-armed Boers, khaki even superseded scarlet for home service in 1902 and the British Army had become very much a modern-looking army.

The pressure to adopt khaki was not felt elsewhere in Europe as uniforms of blue, grey or dark green had never posed such a problem to their wearers, and when the First World War erupted in 1914, both French and German armies wore grey-based, rather than khaki uniforms. Only in the United States, perhaps as a result of its own colonial war in the Philippines, was khaki also specified in 1902 for standard army service dress. As a dye, khaki proved a difficult colour to produce consistently and although the British Army finally solved this, the U.S. Army continued to be dogged by a lack of ability to fix it and right up to the early years of World War Two, U.S. battledress appeared in a variety of tan, brown, and brown-greenish colours. This was one of the main reasons for the adoption of the blueish-green olive drab so characteristic of later U.S. uniforms, although at one time desperate scientists had suggested slate blue as a new combat colour.

Combining the old and the new. The uniform on the right belonged to a sergeant of the 26th Highland Infantry Brigade, part of the 9th Scottish Division fighting on the Western Front between 1914-18. A khaki jacket was worn over the traditional tartan kilt.

Sometimes the kilt might be covered with a khaki apron. Khaki spats, or gaiters, are also shown, being worn over tartan socks.

Tinted photograph of a British soldier on observation duty on the Western Front during the First World War. His khaki webbing equipment is clearly shown.

En Avant!

Above, **Territorial soldier of the Devonshire Regiment posing for a studio photograph c.1914. He wears webbing equipment, including the Mills Webbing Cartridge Belt for carrying ammunition. A young recruit, he has not pulled down his trousers overs his puttees, his chin strap has ridden up beneath his cap badge, and his waist belt is low.**

Top left, **tinted photograph of a French soldier on a postcard. By late 1914, the standard French Army uniform of dark blue jacket and red trousers had been replaced by a uniform coloured Horizon Blue or Tricolour Grey (deriving from the manufacturer blending red, white, and blue in the cloth). The shrapnel helmet was pioneered by the French.**

U.S. troops in France in 1917 wearing olive drab uniforms and Western-style campaign hats. The fact that they are still wearing canvas leggings rather than puttees indicates they have just arrived in the war zone.

HUSSAR TROOPER, REVIEW ORDER.

H. I. M. THE EMPEROR OF GERMANY
IN FIELD-MARSHAL'S UNIFORM, REVIEW ORDER.

STAFF OFFICERS, REVIEW ORDER.

JÄGER OFFICER,
REVIEW ORDER.

OFFICERS, INFANTRY OF THE LINE.
FULL DRESS.   UNDRESS.

FIELD ARTILLERY,
OFFICER AND GUNNER, REVIEW ORDER.

JÄGER (RIFLEMA
MARCHING ORDER

INFANTRY OF THE LINE.

DRUMMER AND PRIVATE, MARCHING ORDER.

GERMAN GREY

The First World War was an enormous trauma for Europe. Some 15 million soldiers and civilians died as a result of it and countless more were physically and mentally scarred. Its awfulness in the minds of those who experienced it and the generations who lived during and after it stems from the shock of modern warfare. For a hundred years previously, there had been no major Europe-wide conflict, the dreadful impact of the Napoleonic Wars had largely been forgotten and absorbed as colourful stories from history, The majority of fighting throughout the 19th century had been colonial campaigns fought around the world and it was here that the first consequences of modern industrial weapons were felt, but it was not on Europeans. Machine guns, repeating rifles, and exploding shells inflicted enormous slaughter on native warriors still fighting with muskets and swords. At the battle of Omdurman in 1898, some 20,000 Sudanese tribesmen were killed or wounded by a British force that suffered only 500 casualties. What was so terrible about the First World War was that this magnitude and efficiency of destruction was visited on European armies by each other.

The reaction to this kind of slaughter inflicted on European cultures was profound. In Britain and France, ultimate victors in the four year struggle against Germany, the mood among its people was not one of absolute triumphant, but a sense that the victory had cost too much, both in lives and material. There was an attempt to exact revenge and reparations from Germany, but after the initial relief and anger had passed, there was a gloomier feeling that the war had been a close run thing, it had not been fought well and that too many sacrifices had been made. Especially in Britain among its ruling classes, the result was anti-militarism, a desire for long-lasting peace, and, above all, a loss of national confidence. The belief grew that Britain was no longer a fighting nation and that Germany, despite having lost the war, was the dominant martial power in Europe. This belief, this national inferiority complex, had been growing in the minds of the British since the second half of the 19th century, when German industry and economy had leaped ahead of its own, and when this power was expressed in a series of brilliant and decisive victories against her neighbours leading to the unification of Germany in 1871.

The power of Germany at the beginning of the 20th century. The uniforms reflect a central European tradition nearer to the Napoleonic era than the practical revolution of British and U.S. campaign dress. The dark blue jackets were replaced with *feldgrau* tunics in 1908.

The sense of defeatism was enhanced by the aggressive performance of the Germans in the First World War and compounded forever in the minds of the world, not only of Britain, by the Second World War. Germany was a natural warrior nation and both Britain and France were better off accepting this and searching for peace whenever possible. It is a belief that continues today at the end of the 20th century and is the motor behind the enthusiasm of many Western Europeans for a United States of Europe. In reality it is a myth. Germany lost both her wars in the 20th century as a result of being outfought by a more efficient and effective Britain and its allies. But it is a myth believed strongly not only by Germany's opponents but by Germany itself. And one of the ways this myth has been enhanced in the minds of so many is through the very appearance of German soldiers. Quite simply, they looked the most martial armed force in the world.

In the middle of the 19th century, Germany was a collection of independent German states. Its soldiers were uniformed in a similar manner as the rest of Western Europe and, indeed, many German states had fought alongside the main powers, especially Britain, during the previous hundred years. Through determined use of economic union, political and military pressure, Prussia united these states under its own leadership in 1871. From this point onwards, German soldiers began to look distinctly different from the rest of Europe. A step towards this separate identity was the development of the *Pickelhaube*, or spiked helmet. Unlike any other military helmet in western Europe, the *Pickelhaube* was a Prussian invention inspired most probably by medieval Prussian helmets. The credit for its invention goes to Frederick William IV, king of Prussia, who reorganised the Prussian army in 1842 and personally designed a new helmet for his soldiers. The 1842 model *Pickelhaube* was high domed with a rear neck guard and front peak and a large brass spike on top. The hat was constructed of thick leather stained black, lacquered and highly polished, while the fittings, including the spike, its base plate, a large Prussian eagle emblem with crown and spread wings, as well as studs and helmet edging, were all of brass. It was impressive, authoritative, and aggressive.

By 1849, 15 other German states had also adopted the *Pickelhaube*, indicating their separate identity with a cockade attached to the side of the helmet and their own heraldic device in place of the Prussian eagle. The national

Early First World War German wool tunic with Brandenburg cuffs bearing rank insignia and piped red. The greenish hue of many *feldgrau* uniforms is clearly visible, more *feld* than *grau*. On the left are two steel helmets plus a suit of body armour issued around 1915 to snipers and sentries, this example having been painted with a camouflage pattern.

colours of the Prussian cockade were black and white. Although quickly becoming popular among German armies, it was not an altogether easy helmet to wear, being somewhat top heavy and prone to falling off in combat. One solution was to reduce its height and this modified style remained in use until 1918. An indication of how seriously other countries were taking the new military developments in Germany, especially after 1871, is revealed by the sudden fashion for the *Pickelhaube* in other armies in the late 19th century, including both Britain and the United States, where it became regular dress wear for many regiments. With the end of Prussian power in 1918, the *Pickelhaube* was abolished in the German army, but its place had already been taken by another form of helmet which is now even more emblematic of German military might.

After a year of modern warfare on the Western Front, all sides were recoiling from the trauma and quickly adapting their equipment to new demands. Parade hats were exchanged for steel helmets, any vestiges of bright colour were exchanged for khaki or grey, and camouflage began to makes it appearance, though primarily for disguising vehicles and artillery. In the German front line, the *Pickelhaube* was at first covered in a grey cloth to subdue its appearance, but by 1915, its hard leather was found to be no protection against shrapnel, one of the biggest sources of death in the trenches, much of it the form of tiny fragments of metal no bigger than a pea. Dr. Friedrich Schwerd, professor at Hanover Technical Institute and a medical consultant to the German Army, recommended the following specifications for a metal helmet: it should weigh no more than 1kg; it should have neck and forehead protection; be made of nickel or manganese steel; be safe against small metal fragments, but not bullet-proof (this would make it too heavy); and be ventilated with two vent lugs; finally, it should be proof against rust and painted.

As manufacturers tackled the design considerations, so the classic German helmet profile emerged with its deep neck guard. Its echoes of medieval German helmets such as the Gothic sallet did not go unappreciated and was later used by propagandists, particularly under the Nazis, who sought to compare German soldiers with the crusading knights of previous centuries. Known as the M1916 *Stahlhelm*, it was an immediate success with trench-assaulting stormtroopers and later became the universal

battlefield helmet for the German Army. An original idea of attaching a steel plate to lugs on the front of the helmet to make it bullet-proof was later abandoned as the extra weight proved unpopular, but the lugs remained another classic element of the overall style. A further design feature was a system of padding inside the helmet to reduce the shock of shrapnel hitting the steel. This consisted of a leather strap riveted at three points to the steel shell to which were attached three cushions stuffed with horse-hair. This also enabled a perfect fit to be obtained for all shapes of head within the six basic sizes. By July 1916, some 300,000 of the new style helmets had been issued and by the end of the war total production was estimated at some 7.5 million. It also became the first item of personal wear worn by a soldier to be camouflaged. At first soldiers improvised, using foliage, sacking, and splodges of paint or mud. In 1917, a white cloth cover was issued for winter fighting and in 1918 a Disruptive Pattern of bold contrasting shapes, which had been used so far to protect vehicles and artillery, was officially adapted to the helmet. Green,

Variety of German spiked *Pickelhaube* helmets emblazoned with the Imperial eagle as well as cavalry variants surmounted by plumes and a brass eagle.

Shrapnel was the biggest killer of soldiers in the First World War and all armies introduced steel helmets. This British soldier at the Somme in 1916 holds up his round steel helmet to reveal a lucky escape.

yellow ochre, and rust brown were painted on in random shapes with a final dusting of sand, while the paint was still wet, to create a non-reflective surface.

After the First World War, the *Stahlhelm* was adopted by other countries, including Austria, Hungary, Bulgaria, and the Irish Free State. It remained the standard German Army helmet throughout the Second World War where its identity with the Nazi regime meant it became deeply unpopular after 1945, surviving only among repressive regimes in South America. Amazingly, after 40 years of notoriety, the essential good design of the *Stahlhelm* was recognised, and despite its Nazi associations, the U.S. Army copied the design for its new kevlar helmet introduced in the 1980s, when it became immediately known as the 'Fritz' and caused some confusion among veterans who had been taught to fire at men wearing such helmets.

Germany entered the Second World War with perhaps the best looking uniform of any European army in the 20th century. Aside from the impressive *Stahlhelm*, its soldiers wore well tailored tunics with four pleated pockets made out of high quality wool, high waisted straight cut trousers, black leather belts and straps and tall leather boots. Overall cloth colour was the traditional German *feldgrau*, which was more green than grey. German officers wore even smarter clothes, including white summer tunics, flared riding breeches and peaked caps. It was a militaristic uniform with echoes of medieval warfare and hunting gear, combined with the sexiness of 19th century parade uniforms, and yet its appearance was not always matched by its battlefield performance.

The German reliance on leather for much of its equipment was a fundamental flaw. The classic marching boots, or 'jackboots' as they became known among the Allies, were expensive and time consuming to make. With wear and exposure to damp, they became loose and wrinkled, prone to causing blistering, and because the vamp overlapped the shaft of the boot it created a ridge which allowed water to collect and seap into the boot. Despite all this, the boots remained popular with their wearers who dubbed them 'dice shakers'. Inevitably, the demands of a losing wartime economy saw the withdrawal of the high boots in favour of ankle boots. Similarly, the leather belts and straps used to support equipment were vulnerable to damp and prone to cracking. The 'Y' strap system of hanging equipment on these straps was itself flawed with loose equipment vulnerable to snagging and making noise, hooks coming loose and bags not being big enough to carry supplies. Overall, it was far inferior to the Allied systems of cloth webbing for supporting equipment and a capacious pack for storing it in. As the war progressed, it was not only leather that was rationed, the generously tailored tunic of the opening years was reduced in length, its pockets lost their pleats and were then reduced to just two, and rayon was substituted for wool. Officers relied more and more on private commissions to maintain their smart appearance. Despite this reality, the myth of the excellence of German uniforms survived the war and even continued to influence other armies, most particularly those of the Soviet Union and its satellite states.

The classic German steel helmet – the *Stahlhelm* – was devised in the First World War. This Model 1918 helmet has the distinctive neck guard and the lug on the side, the side lugs were originally intended to support a steel visor for use by snipers but this was soon abandoned and the lugs remained as ventilation holes.

Model 1918 *Stahlhelm* painted with disruptive pattern camouflage, the first use of camouflage patterns on soldiers' equipment. Prior to this, camouflage patterns had only been used to disguise vehicles.

German stormtrooper soldiers crouch in a trench before an assault in 1918. All these elite soldiers were equipped with the *Stahlhelm*.

DEATH'S HEAD

The German uniform of the Second World War was very much a continuance of 19th century uniform aesthetics, maintained long after other armies such as that of Britain and the United States had exchanged this tradition for practicality, turning uniforms into working clothes. But it was also in Germany in the 1930s that a new, revolutionary use for the military uniform was embraced. It became political and it became the costume of a political elite, the ruling party.

Uniforms had always been associated with politics, right back to their invention in the 17th century, but it was in a subservient role – uniformed soldiers assisting a political power by acting as policemen to suppress and control civilian unrest. When the role of civilian policing was taken over from regular soldiers or the militia by a separate police force, they also wore a uniform based on military designs. But this uniform just served to reinforce their image as servants of politicians who ultimately relied on the consent of the civilian population for their power. In Germany, after 1933, when Adolf Hitler became leader of the nation, uniformed members of his Nazi party were no longer servants of the people but their masters and the uniforms they wore emphasised this control over their very lives.

At heart, Adolf Hitler was a designer. Frustrated in his attempts to become an art student, Hitler put his energy into politics, but his desire to control through design never left him and between political meetings, he would find time to jot down designs for buildings or anything that caught his imagination. Later in his career, he laid claim to designing the swastika emblem of the Nazi party and the original uniform of the SS. Hitler understood the value of symbols in politics and in 1942 explained the reasoning behind his adoption of a new emblem for his party: 'It's not possible to unite the Germanic peoples under the folds of the black-white-and-red flag of the old Germanic Empire – for the same reason as prevented the Bavarians from entering the German Reich, in 1871, under the flag of Prussia. It's the reason why I began by giving the National Socialist Party, as a symbol of the union of all Germanics, a new rallying-sign which was valid also inside our own national community – the swastika flag.'[56]

In 1920s Germany, Hitler's followers were clad in a quasi-military uniform which featured a brown shirt. Hitler had

German *feldgrau* infantry officer wool tunics of World War Two. The grey is now more prominent. The cuff strip was worn by all students and staff officers at military college. The collar insignia of the jacket on the right indicates the wearer was a member of the Waffen SS, the military arm of the Nazi party.

Top, German Iron Cross award for valour made of cloth for wearing on battledress. The Nazi swastika in the centre shows this was worn in the Second World War, indicating the presence of a new political ideology at the heart of the German Army.

been a soldier in the First World War and knew that many of his most active supporters were disaffected veterans who sought the comradeship and order of their army days. A coloured shirt also served as a badge of political affiliation but this basic idea was not Hitler's own. In Italy, Mussolini had clad his own fascist followers in black shirts for their march on Rome in 1922 when they grabbed political power. Known as Black Shirts, the Italian fascists had adopted this from the Arditi, First World War assault troops celebrated for their fearlessness, many of whose disillusioned members later joined the political party. The first official Italian fascist uniform of 1923 consisted of a black shirt and tie, grey-green jacket and breeches, and either a black fez or Alpine cap (the black fez was another Arditi motif).

Hitler claimed not to have been inspired by Italian developments. 'It was in 1921 that I first heard Fascism mentioned,' he recalled. 'The SA (the Brown Shirts) was born in 1920, without my having the least idea of what was going on in Italy. Italy developed in a manner at which I was the first to be surprised.'[57] In fact, Hitler's Brown Shirts developed from the *Freikorps*, groups of veterans from the First World War who assembled into political groups in 1918 to do battle with the forces they considered responsible for their defeat in the war, mainly socialists and communists. This frequently involved street fighting and these political soldiers wore a uniform derived from the Front. It was out of these groups that the Nazi Brown Shirts coalesced. 'I began by creating a service to keep order,' said Hitler, 'and it was only after the bloody brawls of 1920 that I gave these troops the name of Sturm-Abteilung (SA), as a reward for their behaviour.' That title meant Storm Strooper and was a direct reference to the trench-storming soldiers of the Western Front who had won an elite reputation for themselves (just like the Italian Arditi).

Although aligned to Hitler's politics, the reality of the 1920s was that the Brown Shirts owed their loyalty firstly to their immediate commander and Hitler was very well aware of that and established a smaller group of political soldiers loyal only to him. These were the prototype of the SS and he gave them a special uniform. 'I equipped them with a specially designed cap,' he recalled in 1942. 'The skier's cap didn't cost much. It was all done in a very empirical manner. Nothing of that sort was thought out in advance.' The actual uniform consisted of a grey field overcoat, black ski cap with a silver Death's Head button, and black-

Two examples of German World War Two battledress. The camouflage jacket on the right is in 'peas' pattern, a later version of the distinctive tree-inspired camouflage worn exclusively by the Waffen SS. The short jacket on the left is the double-breasted tunic **introduced for wear by Panzer crewmen in tanks and armoured vehicles. Designed not to catch while working inside vehicles, it soon became enormously fashionable and was worn all the time.**

Left, German soldier in combat on the Eastern Front, following Hitler's invasion of Russia in 1941. The overdependence of German soldiers on leather equipment, rather than webbing, meant their battlefield kit was less resistant to the stress and wear of campaign life.

Above, German tank crewman in 1940 wearing the short double-breasted jacket and distinctive panzer beret.

Right, German General Rommel stands on the road to Cairo in 1942. He wears North African issue cotton field tunic and breeches. The use of jodhpur-style breeches worn with boots added to the aristocratic image of German officers, contrasting with the more modern, workaday clothes worn by British and U.S. officers.

bordered swastika armband. This first personal body-guard broke up within a year, but it was quickly followed in 1923 by a new guard called the *Stoßtruppe* Adolf Hitler and they continued to distinguish themselves from the SA Brown Shirts by wearing black. In 1925 this mutated into the *Schutzstaffel*, Protective Squad, or SS, which evolved beyond Hitler's bodyguard into the political police force which ran the entire Nazi regime throughout the 1930s and 40s. Their black uniforms with swastika armbands and Death's Head badges would haunt the whole of Europe as

Front, this became the actual role of the SS as their *Einsatzgruppen*, extermination squads, followed behind the German Army and committed mass executions of Slavs or Jews in a bid to empty the land ready for occupation by German colonists. These horrendous crimes have given the SS Death's Head a particularly chilling association which remains today. This image of ruthlessness was very much the original intention of the Death's Head when it was first adopted by the Nazis, but its brutality at the time was reduced by its association then with a more colourful, and

Germany expanded its political power through war. The political impact of these uniforms did not go unnoticed by the democratic government of the Weimar Republic which sought to ban them. In 1930, Prussia's Minister of the Interior banned the SA's Brown Shirts, but they responded by marching in white shirts with beer-bottle rings as badges.

The Death's Head insignia worn on the collars and caps of SS uniforms has become one of the most sinister aspects of their appearance, casting them in the role of bringers of death. In the Second World War, especially on the Eastern

thus, acceptable past, that of the Prussian Army.

The Death's Head insignia had been worn by Prussian cavalry in the 19th century, most notably the Leib Hussars who wore a predominantly black uniform with a white metal Death's Head, or *Totenkopf* badge, attached to the shako. A black uniform with a Death's Head was also worn by the soldiers raised by the Duke of Brunswick, whose father was a Prussian field marshal. This 'Black Band', as it was nick-named, fought with the British against Napoleon in Spain and at Waterloo. Their motto was 'Victory or Death' and this

Hitler, Göring, and other leading Nazis dressed in the uniform of the Brown Shirts in the early 1930s. The quasi-military style of this civilian outfit created a sense of order and purpose for the political party.

paralleled the 'Death or Glory' motto of the British 17th Lancers who also adopted a Death's Head insignia for their caps; but the regimental origin of this badge claims it was adopted by Colonel Hale, who raised the corps as Dragoons in 1757, and chose the skull and crossbones in commemoration of the death of General Wolfe at Quebec in 1759, with whom he had served. The original Prussian adoption of this emblem may have a more obscure origin, stemming from the endless wars on their eastern frontiers against steppe warriors whose ancient customs included the wearing of the decapitated heads of their enemies as horse decorations. The Germanic Alani of the Crimea were said to take this further by stripping the skins off their enemies and using this as a saddle cloth.

An alternative tradition of the Death's Head is its use by pirates in the 18th century. The first recorded appearance of a skull and crossbones flag on a pirate ship was in 1700 when Captain Cranby of HMS Poole described a French buccaneer as fighting under a 'sable ensign with cross-bones, a Death's Head and an hour glass', the latter indicating that his enemy was running out of time.[58] The use of the Death's Head here may well have been inspired by its widespread symbolic appearance in paintings and prints as a *memento mori*, a reminder of one's mortality. It became highly popular on pirate flags throughout the Caribbean, although its use was meant to indicate that a pirate ship was prepared to give quarter to its victim, whereas a red flag raised was the more fiercesome sign of no quarter. A source nearer to the Nazis in the 20th century was the Italian fascists and here again it appears to have been the influence of the Arditi that provided the inspiration. Along with their black shirts, they carried black flags with silver skulls and in recognition of this, Mussolini had a fringed black banner, with a skull holding a dagger in its teeth, hanging behind his desk at Il Popolo d'Italia. A photograph of 1920 shows a fascist supporter wearing a white metal skull and crossbones badge on his black fez, although this motif would later be supplanted by the *fasces* (a bundle of elm rods with an axe-head protruding at the top – an ancient Roman emblem of justice which was also interpreted as meaning strength through unity) as the main Italian fascist emblem. Whatever the ultimate origin of the Death's Head, it has always been a sign of ruthlessness and the Nazis of the 20th century most certainly added a further layer of barbarity to it.

Top, **Hitler Youth on parade in the early 1930s. The branch of the Nazi Party intended to appeal to young people, the Hitler Youth wore a uniform inspired largely by the British Boy Scout movement.**

Above, **appealing to an even younger audience are these toy paper cut-out figures of Brown Shirt party members carrying Nazi banners c.1935. The extent and effectiveness of Nazi propaganda meant that virtually every aspect of daily life was dressed in Nazi regalia.**

Top, Czapska belonging to an officer of the 17th Lancers c.1855. The regiment's motto was 'Death or Glory' and this hat features the Death's Head. Previous to this, the Death's Head emblem was worn by some German Napoleonic units and was familiar as an emblem of warning on pirate flags.

Top, German Death's Head Hussar painted by E. Dupuis in 1914 for a French postcard of the First World War. The Death's Head as a badge of Prussian cavalry may well have been one of the reasons for its adoption by the Nazi SS, who also considered themselves an elite body of troops.

Top, German peaked cap worn during the Second World War, featuring the Nazi eagle and the Death's Head, the sign of an SS policeman or soldier.

SS insignia and Death's Head painted on an armoured car during the German invasion of Poland in 1939. This use of the Death's Head recalls its earlier appearance on vehicles used by the *Freikorps,* the predecessors of the Nazi party, during the political unrest immediately following the First World War.

The symbolic meaning of the Nazi swastika armband and flag was clear to Hitler: 'in the red we see the social ideal of the movement, in the white the national idea, in the swastika the mission of the fight for the the victory of Aryan man, and at the same time also the victory of the idea of creative work which in itself is and always will be anti-Semitic.'[59] Before Hitler adopted the swastika for the Nazi party, the ancient symbol for the sun (also meaning 'good luck') had already been in use among many fringe German political groups, including the New Templars founded by Georg Lanz von Liebenfels in 1900, devoted to the recreation of pagan rituals and sacrifices. Hitler's one contribution was to reverse the traditional thrust of the symbol so the arms pointed clockwise. Hitler did however design the party banner featuring an eagle on top of the swastika, apparently spending much time in the Munich State Library looking through art books for the correct eagle model. The SS runic insignia originated among the followers of Guido von List who formed the Thule Society, another pagan society aligned with right-wing politics in the 1920s, the lightning double SS meant to symbolise a new racially pure Reich.

In later years, as Hitler became war leader, his involvement in the minutiae of German uniforms and emblems was reduced, but he still maintained an interest in the appearance of his soldiers and mentioned on several occasions his own particular passion for one item of clothing: leather shorts. As a young man in Austria, he wore shorts all the time, regardless of the temperature, and regretted having to stop wearing them as he progressed in German politics. 'The feeling of freedom they give you is wonderful,' he declared. 'Abandoning my shorts was one of the biggest sacrifices I had to make. I only did it for the sake of North Germany. Anything up to five degrees below zero I didn't even even notice… In the future I shall have an SS Highland Brigade in leather shorts.'[60] He had already mentioned the idea to the head of the SS: 'I suggested to Himmler that he might dress two or three guards units in leather shorts.'[61]

By the 1930s, black appears to have become the offical colour of fascist uniforms throughout Europe. Nazi sympathisers and sister parties in other countries all adopted black shirts and uniforms, including the British Union of Fascists. As a counter-balance to the power of the German Army, Hitler created an armed section of the SS known as the *Waffen-SS*. Generally, they wore field clothes similiar to the army, but retained their own insignia. The only German soldiers to have worn black uniforms on the battlefield were the tank crews of the Panzer units. Not only did they wear a black uniform, including cap, but they also wore the Death's Head insignia on their lapels, even though they were not part of the SS, a direct reference to their Prussian cavalry forefathers. They also wore unconventional doublebreasted jackets that were cut especially short over the hips, a practical consideration along with the lack of external pockets so it did not snag on equipment inside a tank. This outfit was very much a battlefield exception and black uniforms remained the sign of a para-military force. After 1945, this association of black with firm, frightening authority has been employed by both repressive and democratic regimes who continue to put armed policemen in black uniforms.

German Afrika Korps soldiers taken prisoner by the British in 1942. Dark glasses are worn alongside light tan cotton shirts and shorts and, for the soldier on the left, calf-length canvas tropical boots, although the lacing proved unpopular with most soldiers who preferred ankle-length versions.

The end of the road for the Nazi Death's Head. A German soldier's skull after the battle for Monte Cassino in Italy in 1944.

East German soldiers on duty in 1990 at the Memorial to Victims of Fascism and Militarism in East Berlin. Their grey uniform with breeches and leather boots demonstrates the profound gap in uniform styles between Soviet and NATO forces, echoing that between the Western Allies and Germany in the Second World War.

Hitler in leather shorts c.1934. Hitler loved wearing shorts and regretted that his political career meant that he could not wear them all the time. He repeatedly asked Himmler to establish an SS Highland Brigade uniformed in leather shorts.

LEATHER JACKET

The leather jacket was born out of the demands of a new kind of warfare in the early 20th century. Men flying in the open cock-pits of aircraft or riding motorbikes as dispatch riders needed protection from the cold winds of high speed. Normal uniforms did not provide this protection and so along with the birth of new military formations such as air corps and motorised units came a new kind of a uniform. Practicality was its spur, but very quickly, like any item of clothing associated with a new elite, it became very fashionable. Among all pilots in the First World War, it was a combination of leather gloves and helmets plus a long leather coat that proved most successful. Dispatch riders, mounted on early motorbikes, tended to wear shorter leather jackets with leather boots. The fashion spread in a limited way to soldiers on the Western Front, stuck in freezing trenches, and some British soldiers wore wool lined sleeveless leather jerkins. Much of this use of leather was unofficial and the clothes were bought privately by individuals who could have it cut and styled to their own requirements, furthering the character of the leather jacket as a sign of individuality and bravado.

In Russia, the early fashion for leather jackets and coats was particularly keen. In the Tsar's army, a black leather *tujurka* was popular in aviation and motorised units, being first introduced in 1912. During the Russian Civil War, all motorised and specialist troops in the Red Army wore outfits of caps, coats, breeches, leggings, and boots, all made of black leather. Variations on this uniform were provided by the armed crews of the armoured trains who wore leather dyed in different colours. The crew of the train that took Trotsky around Russia were clad from head to toe in red leather and were nicknamed the Red Hundred.

In 1918, the zip fastener industry was invented with a major order from the U.S. Navy for 10,000 zips to do up a 'wind-cheating' flying suit. The zip was applied to leather jackets and became a useful item for civilians working outdoors in the 1920s and 1930s. During the Spanish Civil War from 1936-39, as individuals volunteered from many nations for the International Brigades fighting on the side of the Republicans, many brought with them practical, hard-wearing clothes and these included a number of short, zip fastened 'windcheater' brown or black leather jackets. More humble volunteers were issued with the older style

Hermann Göring in 1923 at the very beginning of the Nazi party wearing a long leather coat. Leather coats began as practical wear for drivers exposed to cold winds on motorbikes or in aircraft, but quickly became fashionable beyond their immediate use.

sleeveless British leather trench jerkin. Another practical item favoured by the Spanish militias was the one-piece dungaree overall, usually blue, called a mono.

In the Second World War, the leather jacket remained the preserve of pilots. Sheepskin-lined thick brown leather flying jackets, flying trousers and boots were worn by the RAF and U.S. Air Force, being particularly suitable for the high-altitude long-range bombing raids against occupied Europe. Temperatures during these raids could be savage and gloves had to be worn at all times to prevent hands freezing to the aircraft equipment. Some flying suits were even heated with electrical wires sandwiched between the layers, a little like an electric blanket. Lighter leather jackets with elasticated wrist and waist bands were popular on the ground with American pilots who sometimes had them painted on the back with the kind of jokey images, nick-names and bomb tallies that appeared on the nose sections of aircraft. RAF pilots did not wear their flying jackets off-duty and it is easy to see how the casual glamour of American pilots stationed in Britain added to the sex appeal of the leather jacket.

Aside from the brief appearance of leather waistcoats among the crew of British armoured units, the leather jacket remained unused in Allied armies of the Second World War. Unsurprisingly, the German army was much keener on leather clothes. Using leather equipment long after other armies had abandoned it for more practical webbing, black leather jackets and trousers were worn by Panzer crewmen and U-boat sailors, long leather coats by motorcycle riders, and privately acquired often fur-lined long leather coats were worn by officers. This distinction between the Allied brown leather flying jacket and the German black leather army jacket or coat remained an influence on post-war popular culture. The brown leather jacket became the casual wear of the regular outdoors guy, whereas black leather has become an aggressive, confrontational outfit worn by biker gangs such as the Hell's Angels (who even wore German helmets and Iron Crosses) and rock musicians creating a rebellious image, from early Elvis to punk and heavy metal. Tightly tailored black leather wear has even managed to acquire an aura of unorthodox sexuality, again partly because of its Nazi German associations.

Top, B3 U.S.A.A.F. leather flying jacket with sheepskin lining was a practical item designed to protect World War Two airmen against the cold of high altitudes, but it soon became a favourite item of U.S. servicemen who wore it more frequently on the ground than in the air. Its waterproof lacquer coating rapidly deteriorated.

Above, a leather-jacketed crewman of the U.S. Army Air Corps makes easy friends with an Australian WAAF in Darwin in 1942. Zip fastenings were used widely in all U.S. military clothing, adding to their modern appeal.

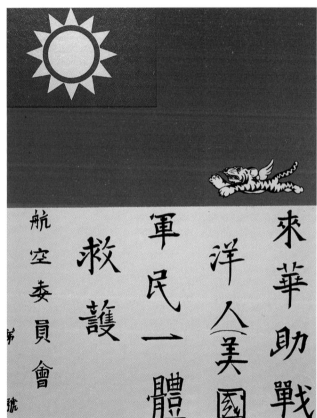

Film poster for *The Wild One* starring Marlon Brando in 1954. Brando, acting as the leader of a gang of lawless bikers, wears the World War Two U.S. flying jacket but turns it into an icon of post-war pop culture and youth rebellion.

'Blood chit' worn on the back of leather flying jackets by U.S. aircrewmen of the Flying Tigers unit operating over China in World War Two. The notice in Chinese states that the wearer of the jacket is friendly and should be taken care of.

WAR AS WORK

A revolution in military uniforms occurred around 1900 and the result was the practical khaki battledress that saw American and British soldiers through the First World War. The move away from creating an impressive and hopefully discouraging impression on an enemy, to a more realistic approach, adapted to long campaigning in which the enemy endeavoured to keep out of rifle range, was confirmed by the horrible experience of the Western Front.

The bitter experiences of First World War veterans, widely publicised in popular books and newspapers, finally removed any sense of glamour from the undertaking of war. Red coats and blue coats were now the stuff of parade grounds and holiday march pasts, when ceremonial dress had already begun to have a whiff of nostalgia about it, evoking past empires and past certainties when a line of red had been enough to disperse a horde of natives. A nation's monarch or president would continue to be guarded by soldiers in bright uniforms, but this merely served to underline the archaic nature of this kind of costume. Uniforms as display had come to the end of the road. Modern uniforms for modern warfare were now to become workclothes for the unglamorous but necessary job of defending one's liberty.

Both Britain and the United States entered the Second World War with uniforms little changed from the khaki battledress of World War One, but as the war progressed it was the U.S. Army, backed by the considerable wealth and advanced industry of its nation's economy, that led the way in creating a brand new style of military uniform which was both comfortable and hard-wearing. Indeed, it brought the efficiency of the American factory-floor to the battlefront and the result was a practical uniform that, ironically, created a whole new glamour for itself as America emerged as a military and cultural superpower. The U.S. Army M41 Field Jacket exemplifies this new attitude. It was the most recognisable item in a whole new concept of military clothing developed by the U.S. Office of the Quartermaster General. Rather than relying on one thick layer of clothing to protect a soldier from the elements, it was realised that several lighter layers could be far more effective, as they trapped warm air beneath the layers and gave greater insulation against cold. Such layers could then be removed if the weather was warmer, thus creating an all seasons, all

U.S. Paratroopers loaded with equipment in North Africa prepare for a drop in enemy occupied territory in Salerno, Italy, in 1943. Every aspect of their uniform has been utilised for carrying equipment. This becomes the new design philosophy for soldiers in the second half of the 20th century.

Opposite, U.S. soldiers in Italy in 1943. The front two wear the popular zippered windbreaker Winter Combat Jacket. This basic pattern, including knitted wool collar, wristlets and waistband with diagonal pockets, has continued to be a best-selling casual item for men and women long after the end of the war.

climates uniform. A basic soldier's outfit would therefore include: wool vest and underpants; wool socks; wool shirt and trousers; wool sweater; pile jacket and trouser liners; windproof outer jacket and outer trousers. To this could be added gloves, scarf, wool hat and overcoat. This principal of layering has since been adopted by all advanced armies and continues today.

The M41 Field Jacket was a key element of this layering system and much effort and money was put into its design. By turning to the civilian sector and examining over 300 commercially made items, it was finally decided that a wind-breaker-style jacket would provide a soldier with both something warm and comfortable and yet lightweight with no great bulk. It was to have a cotton shell of windproof material, a light wool lining, a collar that could be worn up, a generally loose-fit shape, diagonal pockets, both button and zip fastening at the front and tabs on the sleeves and hips to keep out cold air. It was a classic of practicality and instantly gave U.S. soldiers a modern look.

Several design changes and modified versions followed, but essentially the M41 Field Jacket was to be the basic item of the U.S. soldier in Europe and the Pacific and some 23,000,000 were manufactured by civilian contractors. The jacket, however, was not a great hit with soldiers in the field, mainly because the principal of layering was misunderstood. Soldiers wanted it to be warmer and more rain-proof than it was, but they objected to wearing an extra raincoat or overcoat because it was too bulky. Thus the Field Jacket was expected to be an all-purpose coat by itself for which it was not designed. Some U.S. soldiers even adopted the thick British battledress blouse in preference, others simply lined it with newspapers. Failures in battlefield supply also meant that the right combinations of clothing were not always available. The Army Quartermaster took on board these complaints and in 1944 the M43 field jacket was issued. It was longer, had a drawstring at the waist, a detachable hood and four large cargo pockets. Its double layers of sateen cloth had greater wind resistance and a variety of linings could be worn with it, thus replacing five other different types of jackets and coats.

The loose-fit style of these jackets did not look very smart and made its wearers look more like factory-workers than soldiers, something that had bothered the first wearers of khaki jackets back in the middle of the 19th century. Soldiers like wearing smart uniforms. But by the end of the

Posed publicity photograph showing a U.S. mortar crew in Normandy after the Allied D-Day landings in 1944. They wear the standard M1 steel helmet and M41 Field Jacket.

U.S. infantry advance through the snow-covered fields of Belgium during the Battle of the Bulge in January 1945. They wear bedsheets as improvised winter camouflage.

war, as U.S. soldiers liberated European cities, their casual style seemed to embody their easy confidence and affluence, which made them enormously attractive to European women and contributed to a greater interest in casual clothes for all men after the war. Even U.S. Army cotton trousers enjoyed a vogue as 'chinos', their nickname going back to the turn of the century when American soldiers first wore khaki in the Spanish-American War in the Caribbean and the Philippines. *Chino* is a Spanish word meaning 'toasted', a reference to the light brown colour.

Herringbone twill, a tightly woven cotton fabric, was a favourite cloth of the U.S. Army. Its combination of light weight with strength made it a flexible material for use in all terrains and climates, including the demanding environment of the jungle in the Pacific War, as well as being used to protect against gas attacks. It replaced blue denim as the material for one-piece suits worn by army mechanics, as denim was considered to be less durable. It was also dyed with camouflage colours, becoming the material of the first camouflage uniforms worn by the U.S. Army. Shortages in raw materials meant the Quartmaster Corps was forced to consider synthetic textiles with the result that much useful research was carried out, often coming up with superior materials. Nylon replaced silk in parachutes, brass buttons were changed for plastic, rayon was introduced for clothing, and the synthetic waterproofing of raingear was proved to be more effective than rubber treated types.

The strength of advanced armies is the degree to which specialisation has set in. This was reflected in the U.S. Army by the variety of clothes designed for specific tasks. U.S. Paratroopers wore a long jacket in which every aspect of their work seemed to have been considered. Made of water-repellent cotton with a roll collar and four large diagonal pockets with snap fasteners, it even included a zip fastened vertical throat pocket containing a knife for cutting entangled parachute lines. Matching trousers included capacious pockets and tapered legs which could be tucked inside the tall 'jump boots' which featured ankle-support and long laced fronts, all design aspects that not only influenced future military wear but also later civilian casual clothing. Similarly, U.S. tank crewmen had bib-fronted overalls over which they wore a short zippered 'tanker' jacket with knitted wrists and collar, two diagonal pockets, and a knitted waistband that became so popular

British World War Two khaki serge battledress tunics. Sergeant stripes and divisional insignia are attached to the sleeves. Although not part of a layering system, as devised by the U.S. Army, these warm jackets were popular with soldiers, including many U.S. troops who borrowed them from their British allies.

General Dwight D. Eisenhower, supreme commander of Allied forces, stands among the ruins of Berlin in June 1945. The U.S. general liked the smart appearance of the British battle tunic and had the U.S. Army devise their own version, called the ETO wool jacket, which he wears here. It became known as the 'Ike' jacket.

it was worn by generals and anyone who could get hold of it, and is still a best-seller today. The modernist aesthetic of stripped-down utility was beginning to have a fashion appeal all of its own.

British uniform design in World War Two operated in the shadow of the Americans with the vast resources they could bring to bear, but whereas it might have lacked glamour, its effectiveness was very much appreciated by soldiers in the frontline. Continuing its pioneering desire for practicality, the British Army took on various new suggestions for equipment and clothes. A most ingenious idea came from Colonel Rivers-Macpherson who criticised the current webbing system as clumsy, noisy, and prone to get caught on obstacles. He recommended a new item of clothing based on the 'Poacher's Jacket' in which a khaki heavy cotton waistcoat was covered in pockets and slots for containing the items usually attached to webbing. Called the Battle Jerkin, it entered army service in 1942 but enjoyed limited availability, perhaps because the economic demands of war meant already standard material had to be kept in use. It later developed into a skeleton harness used by specialist raiding units. Another innovatory item was the 'A' frame bergen rucksack. Made of khaki canvas it was considerably more capacious than the standard backpack, being used by Commandos who had to carry extra loads of ammunition alongside their usual material. Special forces also made use of the water-resistant Denison Smock. The only camouflaged item worn at that time by the British Army, it incorporated a zip fastening and elasticated wristbands.

Standard British Battledress consisted of a two-part combination of blouse and trousers in khaki serge. Designed in 1937, it replaced the khaki Servicedress which had been worn since 1907. As wartime economies bit into uniform production, a second 'utility' version of the Battledress appeared in 1942 removing all unnecessary refinements such as pocket pleats and fly fastening of the blouse front. A new form of headgear called the Universal Pattern Field Service Cap consisted of a simple serge brimless cap usually worn at a jaunty angle on the head. Despite other armies introducing new style helmets with neck guards, such as in Germany and the United States, the British Army continued to use the round 'battle-bowler' typical of the First World War. Improvements were made to webbing, making it lighter and more flexible, carrying its load above the waist so as to improve mobility. Denim over-alls were issued to be worn over Battledress for laborious tasks, but its lighter weight made it a warm weather alterna-tive to serge and it was often worn in combat. Thick woollen greatcoats completed the basic outfit, the British answer to the American layered approach. One aspect of British Battledress that did impress the Americans, however, was the smartness of its short jacket and, after General Eisenhower's personal intervention, this was the inspiration behind the ETO wool jacket issued in 1943 which remained a much favoured alternative to frontline clothes, giving back to U.S. soldiers some of the elegance of the parade ground.

By the end of the Second World War, the three main allies, Britain, the United States, and Russia, had emerged victorious over the considerable military challenges of Germany and Japan. In the six years of their struggle, they had transformed themselves from armies with their feet still in the First World War to wholly modern 20th century forces, and as such, in the following 50 years to the end of the 20th century, little changed in their appearance. The basic uniform lessons learnt in the Second World War continued to dominate the conflicts of the Cold War. American soldiers in Korea and Vietnam still wore a battledress similar to that of 1945. Britain continued to wear a similar wartime outfit throughout its many end of empire campaigns. The least advanced of the major powers was the Soviet Army, which continued to follow a uniform style similar to their German foes and thus, after 1945, always looked a little more archaic that its rivals, placing more emphasis on the old militaristic virtues of leather and well tailored jackets and trousers. When one viewed their client states, an East German soldier looked almost identical to a Nazi stormtrooper, whereas West Germans followed the American-style of NATO. The major change to take place in this period was the adoption of camouflage pattern material uniforms by all major armies from the 1960s onwards.

U.S. and Russian soldiers meet at Torgau on the Elbe in April 1945. These two soldiers exemplify the broad contrast between the Western open-neck casual and Soviet buttoned-up militaristic uniform styles which continued to set the tone for both armies after 1945 during the Cold War.

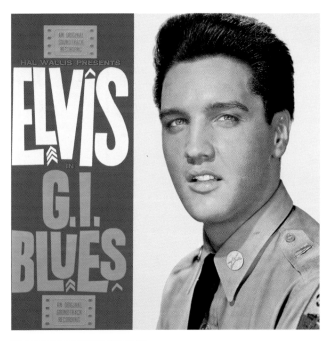

Record sleeve for *G.I. Blues* by Elvis Presley in 1960. When Elvis did his military service in West Germany, he set the seal on the popular appeal of U.S. military clothes which continued to dominate male casualwear long after the end of World War Two.

WOMEN'S UNIFORMS

Women have always been associated with armies, largely in an unofficial role as camp followers or the wives of soldiers allowed to live in camp. Some women have even pretended to be men to enrol and fight alongside their male comrades, but it was not until the middle of the 19th century that the presence of women was officially recognised and they were allowed to wear a uniform especially designed for them. It was the *vivandières* of the French Army that paved the way.

Carrying little barrels of brandy at the battle front and in camp, *vivandières* were regarded as both suppliers of refreshments and potential nurses. There was no sexual ambiguity about their presence, they were expected to exhibit good moral behaviour and were frequently married to men in the ranks. In order to overcome any doubt in this quarter, they were allowed to wear uniforms based on those of the regiment they served in. The most colourful *vivandières* were those serving in the newly raised Zouave regiments, the masculine appearance of the men's uniforms being modified by wearing a skirt over the baggy breeches, but the jackets and other equipment remained basically the same. Serving in the Crimean, Italian, and Mexican campaigns of the French Army, many *vivandières* followed their regiments to the battle front and some performed bravely under fire. Antoinette Trimoreau of the 2nd Zouaves and Jeanne-Marie Barbe of the Guard Zouaves both received Military Medals during the battle of Magenta, Antoinette saving the regimental eagle standard.

Just as the fashion for Zouaves was taken up by volunteer regiments in the American Civil War, so the idea of the *vivandière* was adopted by American women who chose to serve with their men at the battlefront. A contemporary description of *vivandières* in the Confederate regiment of Coppens' Louisiana Zouaves records them wearing: 'a pair of high heel shoes, over the top of which shine white gaiter tops; above these are tight fitting pieces of leather extending to the knee; there they unite with red, wide drawers; they have a blue skirt with red border from waist to their knee and a blue jacket from waist to neck.'[62] Their presence among soldiers caused much popular interest and one *vivandière* performed on stage to raise money for a sick soldier. 'She is a very strong looking woman and tells with perfect nonchalance of killing Yankees and the like,' recalls a theatre critic of 1861. 'The children crowded to see her,

Countless of Athlone (left) and corporal in the Women's Transport Service during World War One. Khaki jacket with long khaki skirt was the typical uniform worn by women serving in the British armed forces at this period.

dressed as she was in the gay costume of her vocation.'[63] The most celebrated Civil War *vivandière* was 'French Mary' or Mary Tepe. A French immigrant, she followed her husband into the army and ended up in the 114th Pennsylvania Zouaves where she exhibited great courage under fire, being wounded during the siege of Fredericksburg. For her gallantry in action, she was awarded the Kearny Cross.

The increasing ferocity of industrialised warfare from the middle of the 19th century to the First World War meant the presence of women as nurses was increasingly welcome and necessary. The Red Cross, founded in 1864 specifically to look after battlefield wounded, devised their own uniform for nurses and these were later joined by many other uniformed nursing agencies equipped for frontline duty. In 1907, the First Aid Nursing Yeomanry was established in London as a volunteer organisation providing medical service for mounted troops and they wore a khaki uniform when serving as ambulance drivers and nurses in the First World War. The original thought behind this particular organisation was to provide a more positive vision of female contribution to society in contrast to the radical suffragettes. Because the First World War took such a toll of manpower, women began to be recruited for other roles as well, all non-combatant, but vital to maintaining military efficiency. In the British Army, the Women's Army Auxiliary Corps was formed in 1917. In 1918, this was re-named Queen Mary's Army Auxiliary Corps, but as soon as the war was over it was disbanded. Their uniform consisted of a khaki broad-brimmed hat and a long khaki dress over black stockings and shoes. No further role for women in the army was envisaged until another war seemed imminent in the late 1930s.

In Britain in 1938, the Auxiliary Territorial Service was formed and some 80,000 ATS women served as cooks, drivers, postal and storage workers, and administrative staff. Their official army status, however, was not recognised until 1941 with the introduction of the Defence (Women's Forces) Regulations which finally integrated them into the regular army, thus giving them the same privileges and international protection given to male soldiers. From 1938, the ATS had worn a khaki uniform of shirt, tie, cap, jacket, and skirt, but their rank badges and titles were not the same as the regular army until 1941 when they were allowed similar rank badges to their male colleagues,

Recreated member of the Auxiliary Territorial Service in 1940. She wears the ATS serge battle dress with the addition of a steel helmet, service respirator and haversack.

ATS members fire an anti-aircraft gun during World War Two. They wore combat clothes virtually identical to male battledress, including trousers, and their officers were accorded the respect of being saluted by their male comrades, who did not usually do this for the ATS.

although the receipt of salutes from male soldiers was not so forthcoming. A battledress uniform with trousers was issued to ATS members when on Anti-Aircraft gun sites and here they were also accorded the recognition of being saluted by junior male ranks. After the war, the ATS was absorbed into the Women's Royal Army Corps, but in 1992 this was disbanded as women now served alongside men throughout the British Army and thus no longer needed a separate uniform.

In the United States, the Women's Army Auxiliary Corps was founded in 1942. Like the ATS, it took a little longer for this unit to be officially absorbed into the U.S. Army, when it became known as the Women's Army Corps in 1943. Again, like the ATS, it began as a non-combatant pool of labour, but as the war progressed women found themselves in the zone of battle. Members of the Women's Army Corps waded ashore at Normandy and followed their male colleagues into Nazi-occupied Europe. Serving in these battle zones meant that the WAC were provided with the work-style battledress typical of the U.S. Army but the jackets and thick woolen trousers of their male colleagues were found to be unsuitable and the U.S. Office of the Quartermaster General designed clothes specifically for them, incorporating their layering concept of several lighter items of clothing. Male items that remained unchanged for use by women included the steel helmet, combat boots, and the backpack. One apparently important aesthetic concern was that the breast pockets on women's shirts would not be used and these were substituted with false breast pocket flaps. Today, in the U.S. Army, women serve alongside men in identical clothes.

Recreated U.S. Women's Army Corps member wears the olive drab field uniform introduced in 1943. Similar to male combat wear, it includes the M1 helmet, a respirator, M36 pistol belt and M36 pack with blanket roll.

CAMOUFLAGE

Modern camouflage – the use of painted or printed patterns to deceive the enemy – was first devised in the First World War to conceal artillery positions from spotter aircraft. It was later adapted to the disguise of vehicles, tanks, aircraft and ships. The original idea was a chameleon-style approach in which the camouflage pattern mimicked its surroundings so the gun position merged into the landscape, but when camouflage was applied to moving objects a new concept was born, the Disruptive Pattern.

More akin to the camouflage of tigers and zebras, disruptive pattern uses boldly contrasting shapes of light and dark colours to create a confusing effect, breaking up the predictable silhouette of an object, so an enemy can neither recognise it fully or aim its weapon completely on the fractured object. Although most vehicles were painted with camouflage by the end of the First World War, the idea had not yet embraced the ordinary soldier who continued to wear either khaki or grey into battle. The only exception to this were the new German steel helmets which were sometimes painted with a bold disruptive pattern of many colours, perhaps inspired by the lurid camouflage schemes on German aircraft.

Immediately after the war, several countries experimented with the use of camouflage for soldiers' clothing, but it was not until the 1930s that camouflage pattern uniforms were devised and even then in a very limited capacity. It was in Nazi Germany that this development first occurred. Professor Otto Schick designed a series of tree-inspired patterns for the *Waffen-SS*, the military arm of the SS. These patterns appear to have been based on the effect of dark green bark peeling off a trunk to reveal contrasting shapes of light brown wood beneath. Leaf shapes were then added to this to create a green and brown forest pattern which could be worn in a reversable version in which either the 'autumn' brown or 'spring' green predominated. Bearing in mind the mystical affinity of Germans for the forest out of which they believed they were born, it is not surprising that such a choice of tree and leaf motifs should have been accepted by the SS, who saw itself as an organisation on the verge of creating a pagan culture in which a traditional reverence for nature would form the basis of a new German religion. In contrast, the German army adopted a completely separate, machine-orientated

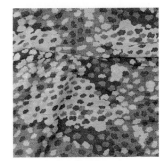

Top, three early experiments in U.S. camouflage uniforms carried at Fort Ethan Allen in Vermont in 1942.

Above, one of the earliest published examples of soldiers in completely camouflaged uniforms. Illustration from a French essay on camouflage c.1920.

Top, sleeve of German camouflage smock, early 1940s, showing the most literal Waffen-SS tree pattern. Given a post-war name of 'palm tree' pattern, it is more likely based on the leaves of the ash tree. *Above,* World War Two German combat trousers in the so-called 'peas' pattern, a later version of the German tree patterns, introduced in 1944.

Top left, German reversible pattern of the 1940s mimicking clusters of oak leaves, this side spring green.

Top right, Leopard skin pattern worn by elite troops of the Zaire regime. Many African army patterns are less about camouflage than about distinguishing particular units.

Middle top left, British Disruptive Pattern devised in the 1960s and still used today by the British Army.

Middle top right, Finnish pattern of the 1960s.

Middle bottom left, French brushtroke pattern of the 1950s, used by French troops in Vietnam and possibly the inspiration behind the indigenous Tigerstripe pattern used by the South Vietnamese Army.

Middle bottom right, Swiss army pattern used from the 1960s to 1994, based on a rare German pattern of the 1940s, now popularly worn in street fashion trousers.

Bottom left, South Vietnamese Tigerstripe pattern of the 1960s became popular with U.S. Special Forces stationed in Vietnam who even adapted it to swimming trunks.

Bottom right, French desert pattern used during the Gulf War in 1991.

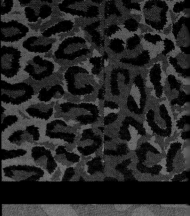

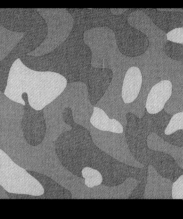

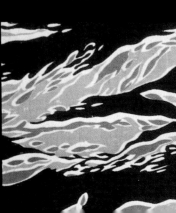
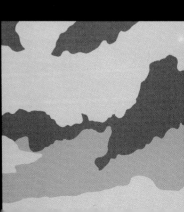

scheme of splinter shapes in green, light and dark brown with a falling rain motif printed over it, firstly being used on tents, then being incorporated into battledress. Both types of patterns were used throughout the Second World War.

Britain did very little to respond to this new style of uniform, but both the United States and the Soviet Union devised their own camouflage patterns. The U.S. Army adopted a frog-skin pattern of either green or brown random shapes which was mainly used in the Pacific war and not in Europe, partly because it made soldiers wearing it look like Germans, and partly because it proved unpopular with soldiers who considered it had little effect one way or the other. The Soviet Army utilised several patterns, but the most characteristic were large jig-saw shapes of contrasting colours. German innovation in the use of camouflage did not stop with its forest patterns. To disguise its soldiers against the new threat of infrared sights which could see at night, special dyes were devised to make some colours reflectant in infrared so the disruptive pattern effect was maintained. These have subsequently been adopted by all modern armies and, in a modified form, are still incorporated today in camouflage material.

After the Second World War, camouflage briefly disappeared as the threat of war appeared to have gone and armies braced themselves for a period of guarding borders. The first conflicts of the Cold War saw the Americans and their allies still fighting in khaki, but by the war in Vietnam a new sensibility had taken grip. In the 1950s, the French pioneered a camouflage pattern consisting of brushtroke shapes, perhaps in turn inspired by the very limited use of a similar pattern by the British on the Denison Smocks used by their Special Forces. French paratroopers in Vietnam wore this brushstroke pattern and later South Vietnamese forces invented their own similar pattern, characterised by black horizontal brushstrokes, which became known as Tigerstripe. This proved popular with the U.S. Special Forces serving as advisors in Vietnam, who at the beginning of the war were reduced to privately buying 'Duck Hunter' pattern camouflage goods from sporting outlets such as Sears and Roebuck. By the mid-1960s, the U.S. Army had overcome its earlier reservations regarding the usefulness of camouflage and devised their own patterns, the most long-lived being the Woodland pattern of brown and green vaguely leaf-inspired shapes which continues in a modified form today. The British Army finally adopted a camouflage

Recreated U.S. Special Advisor to South Vietnamese Rangers during the Vietnam War c.1965. He wears the early version of the Woodland pattern that has since become the primary U.S. Army camouflage. His helmet is painted with the Ranger's tiger insignia.

U.S. troops in 'chocolate chip' desert pattern worn during the Gulf War. Despite being scientifically devised for the best protection, this pattern did not prove popular with soldiers and was later replaced with a more simple pattern that deleted the pebble motif.

uniform in the 1970s based on a brushstroke pattern.

By the 1970s, a new heraldry had accidentally evolved in which nations could not only be identified by their distinctive camouflage clothes, but their military affiliations and super-power patronage could also be deduced from the patterns they wore. Warsaw Pact troops of Eastern Europe tended to wear patterns similar to that of their Soviet Russian masters, as did African and Middle Eastern client states. Latin American and Asian allies of the United States tended to wear versions of the U.S. Woodland pattern, except where a strong sense of independent nationalism dictated they invent their own patterns or create versions of the Vietnamese Tigerstripe. French African states wear brushtroke patterns and some former British colonies can be seen in British material. A further laying of meaning was clearly intended when Arab armies adopted Nazi German-inspired patterns in their wars against Israel.

By the 1980s, the U.S. Army updated its image as the leading technological military power by adopting new patterns based on scientific research. Previously, almost all patterns had been invented intuitively by a combination of artists and military personnel. A night-time desert pattern based on a grid was created to confuse night-vision devices, while a new desert pattern was introduced consisting of pebble motifs against light and dark browns, instantly dubbed 'chocolate chip'. But like previous U.S. patterns, it proved unpopular with soldiers and was replaced by a less distinctive pattern of light green and light and dark browns. With the collapse of the Soviet Union, old Soviet patterns were out for the new Russian Army, although they continued to be used by impoverished border guards and militia. A whole array of new patterns were adopted by former Soviet-dominated states who saw the creation of a new pattern as almost as important as a new national flag. In Central Europe, a reunited and resurgent Germany wears a forest-inspired pattern similar to that worn by the *Waffen-SS*, but hopes it will be adopted by a European Defence Force and thus assuage its wartime associations. Britain has no plans to ditch its 30 year old pattern as a step towards further European integration.

Despite the increasing sophistication of camouflage clothing in Western armies, proof against night-vision and infrared, there is still a need to return to the very basics of camouflage as practiced by primitive hunters, the origina-tors of the concept. Special Forces troops, such as the

U.S. Special Forces team on patrol in Vietnam c.1970. In addition to their camouflage clothing, they have smeared their faces with camouflage cream to reduce their visibility.

British S.A.S., are adept at these skills. The main aim is to break up the silhouette of the soldier and the equipment he is carrying. This can be achieved by grabbing handfuls of grass, ferns, or twigs and placing them in the straps attached to helmets and equipment, but such foliage will soon die and change colour, leaves curling up, so a more effective form of shape-distorting camouflage is 'scrim', strips of dull brown and green cloth which are fixed to helmets and equipment, softening the silhouette. The most complete version of this form of camouflage is the 'ghillie suit', named after the Scottish gameskeepers who pioneered it, which consists of hundreds of strips of scrim attached to every part of a soldier's uniform. Especially favoured by snipers waiting motionless for their targets, the 'ghillie suit' is remarkably effective, making soldiers disappear into foliage at a few paces distance. On equipment with which a good grip is essential, such as a gun, scrim is not recommended, instead green masking tape is used to disrupt its characteristic shape.

Human skin is a great give away, not only its pale colour in contrast to a dark uniform, but also the shine of sweat and the readily identifiable pattern of facial highlights. Camouflage creams have been used since the Second World War and are worn by all colours of soldiers, the most important aspect being to alter the usual pattern of highlights. A dark cream is applied to cheeks, chin, and nose, while a light cream is added to parts of the face normally in shadow. Broad slashes of camouflage skin cream are recommended for jungle, vertical slashes for northern forests of conifers, thin slashes in a desert, and big splodges for European deciduous forests. Mixing the cream with spit and earth helps to blur the pattern and the mixture must be applied to every aspect of skin, including eyelids, neck, and hands.

The use of camouflage cream is perhaps the most aggressive visual aspect of a soldier's uniform today, giving him the appearance of a man in a mask on the verge of combat and as such removed of a layer of humanity and responsibility. In Vietnam, the use of face paints seemed to symbolise a step away from civilisation into the barbarity of jungle warfare. This effect has been further exploited by Special Forces soldiers who in urban combat situations exchange camouflage cream for a black rubber respirator proof against gas and smoke and a black flame-resistant hood, both creating a terrifying mask. The S.A.S., along with other Special Forces, has returned to the concept of a military uniform as a fear-provoking medium, first understood by warriors in armour and animal skins and later revived by Nazi soldiers in black with the death's head insignia. The message is clear – resistance is futile – these men are professional killers.

Surprisingly, camouflage patterns have become fashionable in the 1990s as street and club wear, worn by a young generation tired of the predictable youth looks of denim and leather. Such an adoption of military clothing is similar in its unspoken philosophy to that of the early appeal of the leather jacket, in that its military associations are not a sign of young people enthralled by the glamour of war, like their predecessors in the 19th century, far from it. It is a sign of rebelliousness, an anti-fashion statement in which the accepted styles of popular civilian fashion are rejected as trivial and exploitative. Instead, the practical, no-nonsense, hard-wearing qualities of military clothes are embraced as an indication of something beyond the normal boundaries of polite society. Just as denim was accepted by the world in the 1960s and 70s as a sign of freedom from the conformity of the nine-to-five job (and indeed in former Communist countries was embraced as a very real sign of capitalist freedom), so camouflage has emerged as the new denim of the 1990s, worn by a young generation prepared to 'fight' for its freedom from legal, political, sexual and environmental restrictions.

Camouflage as 1990s civilian street clothes, expressing both practicality and an anti-fashion attitude. This man wears U.S. Woodland-style pattern trousers.

Post-1945 sleeve unit insignia badges:

Top left, U.S. Green Berets Vietnam patch
Top right, 9th U.S. Marines 'Hell In a Helmet' 2nd Battalion patch
Middle top left, 1st U.S. Air Cavalry Vietnam Assault patch
Middle top right, U.S. Marines 1st Reconnaissance Battalion patch
Middle bottom left, 9th U.S. Marines 'The Walking Dead' 1st Battalion patch
Middle bottom right, U.S. Special Forces in Grenada Invasion of 1983 patch
Bottom left, 4th U.S. Marines 'The Magnificent Bastards' 2nd Battalion patch
Bottom right, Soviet KGB State Security patch.

REVOLUTION IN MATERIALS

The 1980s saw the predominance of technology in warfare in the form of computer-guided weapons, robotics and advanced information systems. The United States was the undisputed master of this kind of warfare and it was the rush to increase research and expenditure on this new form of warfare that demonstrated to the Societ Union the flaws in its economy, eventually leading to its collapse. In 1991, the promise of all this investment was clearly delivered in the Gulf War when the United States and its allies over-whelmed the powerful army of Iraq in a 24-hour-a-day non-stop campaign of air-raids, missile attacks and lightning tank warfare, all co-ordinated by satellites and computers. The gap in performance between this army of the 1990s and one equipped with weaponry just ten years older could be compared only to that of the British army at Omdurman, 100 years earlier, in which an industrially armed force anni-hilated one little changed from the Middle Ages.

Such a leap in military evolution seems to demand a simi-lar transformation in the appearance of soldiers, but, on the face of it, this is not necessarily so. Western soldiers seem little changed over the last 20 years, some of them would not even seem out of place in 1945. But a revolution has taken place in the invisible world of materials, the stuff out of which uniforms are now made. In the early 1980s, the U.S. Army replaced its traditional steel combat helmet with a new helmet made out of a synthetic material called Kevlar. Kevlar was invented in 1971 by the Du Pont company and is weight for weight five times stronger than steel. Composed of moulded fibres, a Kevlar helmet is impregnated with PVB phenolic resins for rigidity. In tests it proved 30 per cent safer for a soldier in combat than steel and yet weighs far less and is more comfortable to wear. In reflection perhaps of this scientific dimension, the new U.S. helmet was called the Personnel Armour Systems Ground Troops or PASGT. The British Army followed this development with its own replacement for the steel helmet made out of ballistic nylon manufactured by Courtaulds Aerospace, but stopping penetration is not the only problem solved by this new helmet, the kinetic energy of a high velocity bullet can be just as fatal and so a trauma lining has been placed inside the helmet to reduce the impact of a shell fragment or small arms round.

Throughout the age of uniforms described in this book,

British S.A.S. soldiers storm the Iranian Embassy in London to release hostages from terrorists in 1980. They wear synthetic material body armour, flame-retardant black uniforms, respirators, and anti-flash hoods. Despite being worn for practical reasons, their overall appearance is clearly fear-provoking.

body armour had almost disappeared, soldiers putting their trust in the power of their rifles and artillery rather than depending on shields or breastplates. In the early 20th century it made only sporadic appearances in the form of armour for snipers in the First World War or to protect the aircrew of bombers against anti-aircraft fire, or flak, in World War Two. With the revolution in synthetic materials, body armour has returned as an essential aspect of a soldier's equipment and uniform. The U.S. army pioneered its use in Vietnam with flak jackets and in the 1980s it was introduced as standard combat wear. Lagging behind the Americans, the British Army finally introduced body armour for all its troops during the Gulf War in 1991. There are two main types of body armour: one is made from Kevlar and is incorporated into the U.S. Army PASGT vest, the other comprises ceramic plates which use their unique sponge-like chemistry to disperse the kinetic energy of a high velocity bullet. Both types of armour are concealed inside waistcoat style vests covered in standard camouflage material. The British company Courtaulds Aerospace has devised a compound known as Ceramid which is composed of layers of aramid/nylon sandwiched together, which are then sealed in self-contained panels which can be added in pouches to increase or decrease the effectiveness of an armoured vest. Such vests are now usually secured by the use of Velcro straps, another recent development improving on traditional straps and buckles. The effectiveness of U.S. Kevlar body armour has been demonstrated in tests in which it can defeat both 9mm full metal jacket and .44 Magnum rounds fired at 1,400 feet per second.

The revolution in materials has also been applied to the very fabric of combat dress. In 1995, the British Army introduced a new combat kit based on the layering system first developed by the U.S. Army in World War Two. With British and other Western forces increasingly faced with combat zones of widely differing climates and terrain, the new British uniform is intended to be one system of clothing which can be added to as conditions demand. No longer will soldiers have to wait to be issued with specialist tropical or winter fighting gear – the one outfit will do, with additional garments supplied as part of the same range. In the Falklands War of 1982, the chaos caused by soldiers having to be issued with specialist cold weather gear was evident when 2,000 sets of Arctic trousers were made available, but only 1,000 sets of Arctic smocks to go with them. Traditional materials such as leather for gloves and cotton gaberdine for the new combat jacket demonstrate that some things cannot be improved on, but the two-piece rain suit worn over the Soldier 95 kit is an example of the leap forward in materials. At its heart is Gore-Tex, a fabric first devised in 1976, which incorporates a membrane that stops water entering the material but allows sweat to evaporate through it. The Gore-Tex membrane is composed of pure expanded polytetrafluoroethylene and an oleophobic or oil-hating substance which together create a membrane that contains nine billion microscopic pores per square inch – these pores are 20,000 times smaller than a water droplet, but 700 times larger than a molecule of water vapour from perspiration. Thus, rain just rolls off the fabric, while a soldier can still move and perform without becoming drenched in his own sweat. Such materials have radically improved the capability of soldiers to operate in all environments.

British soldier wearing Combat Soldier 95 uniform. It features body armour consisting of either Kevlar or ceramic panels secured by Velcro, a combat suit made out of cotton and polyester, and a helmet made out of ballistic nylon. The camouflage is British DPM and can be made waterproof with the addition of a Gore-Tex layer.

U.S. airborne soldier lands with all his equipment on a military exercise. He wears the U.S. helmet adopted in the 1980s made out of a synthetic material called Kevlar which is far stronger than steel yet much lighter. The German shape of the helmet has had its critics, but demonstrates the design efficiency of the *Stahlhelm*.

FUTURE UNIFORMS

The battlefield of the future is inhabited by strange crea-
tures. RAPTORS, giant pilotless gliders powered by solar
cell batteries, will launch TALON missiles to intercept
enemy missiles as soon as they take off. BATS, missiles
equipped with four wings, will hover over ground targets,
decide which is the weakest point, then strike home.
PROWLERS, robot jeeps, will see through infrared and
video eyes, while ARNOLD, a tank turret mounted on a
robot vehicle, will fire a metal dart at 2.5 kilometers per
second from its electro-magnetic gun, the speed alone
destroying its target. Finally, and most bizarrely of all, an
army of robot insects will be crammed with computer
power and sent against enemy communication centres,
crawling into cables and weaponry, chewing through wires
and short-circuiting their electrical systems.

These and many other weapons are already in development, creating a scenario in which soldiers will be reduced,
perhaps gratefully, to being mere programmers of robot
fighters on a future battlefield, but the reality of a purely
automated war zone is far from likely. Human beings need
to take possession of conquered land and the human face
of a soldier is needed to deliver aide to refugees and
present a friendly, reassuring gesture to a defeated people.
Only humans can win the hearts and minds of the enemy.
The human soldier, therefore, will continue to be an important presence on the battlefields of the 21st century, but the
environment he performs in will have its own demands and
research is being carried out by government departments
and commercial manufacturers on how best to equip him.

Most research favours a completely closed helmet for the
soldier of the future. Equipped with a retractable visor, the
visor is light sensitive so as to protect against sudden
flashes as well as serving to seal the helmet against chemical and biological weapons, a breathing filter being part of
the helmet. Taking inspiration from the helmets of pilots, a
form of Head Up Display might be adopted to help weapon
targetting, although a soldier on the battlefield needs to be
aware of more than just one target and this degree of
concentration might be deemed dangerous.
Communications will be contained within the helmet with
ear pieces linked to other soldiers and a mouthpiece that is
not only linked into this network, but can also be projected
to outsiders with a voice-box possessing a translating

**Soldier of the 21st century as
imagined by the British
electronics company Scicon.
This is a fully integrated combat
suit and helmet with onboard
computers controlling weapons
and suit performance.**

device attuned to the country he is fighting in. For communicating to a commander, a low light television camera could be mounted on the soldier's helmet, so a general finally sees the battlefield from the soldier's perspective.

The combat suit of a future warrior will maintain the concept of a unified and integrated system, taking the form of an armoured vehicle crewman's one-piece uniform. It will be sealed against outside agents and will be designed specifically for the use of the man wearing it. Smart materials will act like a skin, sandwiching a layer of capillaries which could heat or cool the soldier, much like the filaments included in the suits of U.S. pilots in World War Two, a battery pack on the back of the soldier providing the power. Flame-retardant and water-proof textiles are already available, but the real revolution could take place in the field of camouflage. One researcher has suggested that light sensitive microdots could be placed in the surface of the material to enable the combat suit to respond to the colour of its environment just like a chameleon. Sarah Taylor, a lecturer at the Scottish College of Textiles, has devised a method of weaving optical fibres to produce a cloth that changes colour. The British Defence Clothing and Textiles Agency has taken this on board for use in the army. 'One way it might work would be for a sensor to feed an image of a change in background to a microprocessor,' suggests Professor Colin Lewis of the Defence Agency. 'The microprocessor would send an electric impulse to a light-emitting diode which emits different colours. This would be fed to the optical fibres, making the soldier's uniform change colour.'[64] The U.S. Army is currently exploring the use of microscopically thin optical fibres to detect an incoming laser or chemical attack.

Ever since the Second World War, camouflage manufacturers have been forced to consider the non-visual battlefield as well as the visual landscape. Moving beyond the use of infrared reflectant dyes, Thermal Imaging has become a greater threat on the battlefield, detecting the very body heat of a soldier. Camouflage scientists are now seeking to reduce this heat signature in two main ways, either by deceiving the detector or by reducing the overall body heat of a soldier. Shiny, metallic surfaces lose heat more slowly and so by incorporating a layer of shiny material sandwiched between traditional camouflage material, a Thermal Imager will only see the shiny surface and thus be deceived into detecting a lower heat signature. A shiny,

transparent visor could thus shield a soldier's face as well, but such a material making heat loss difficult would also make the soldier uncomfortable, unless he was fitted with the kind of heat controlling capillary system suggested earlier. The other method is one adopted in nature in which a greater body surface helps to release body heat, hence an elephant's big ears. By cladding a soldier in a uniform not dissimilar to the traditional ghillie suit with numerous fins or strips of material, his body heat would be dissipated more efficiently and he would resemble more closely the heat of his environment, but such a solution would have a revolutionary impact on the appearance of a soldier and his uniform, and probably would not be acceptable to him, the aesthetic qualities of a uniform being as important in the 21st century as it has been for the last three centuries.

To complete the protective quality of the combat suit, gloves and boots would form a hermetic seal with the rest of the suit. Essential equipment would be carried in pouches on the suit as well as on a waistbelt. The pockets would contain syringes and medicine to combat wounds and chemical attacks, while self-adhesive patches would be stored to repair any tears in the suit. A miniature laser designator could be attached by Velcro strips to the arm and this could be used to direct artillery and missile attacks on the enemy, thus giving an individual soldier the ability to execute massive fire-power. Global Positioning Navigational Systems have already revolutionised the ability of vehicles to operate in remote areas by calling on a system of satellites and there is no reason why a similar system should not be available to a soldier, giving him instant information on his precise location. Body armour will continue to be worn, but moulded more closely to an individual's fit, thus saving on weight and giving more flexibity. Kevlar and Ceramic armour might be supplanted by a different synthetic compound based on the silk of spiders' webs, said to be stronger than steel but a fraction of the weight.

The soldier of the future will undoubtedly look like a soldier and his uniform will still consist of a helmet and a combat suit and he will most certainly carry a rifle. Despite an array of forms and materials over the centuries, a soldier's clothes will continue to perform the main functions expected of them in the 17th century: to identify, to discipline, to impress, and to give the soldier the confidence to do what he has always been expected to do – to die in the defence of his people.

Reconstruction of how a soldier of the European Defence Force might look in the early part of the 21st century, painted by Stephen Andrew. The visor of his helmet is raised to allow him to use the monocular targetting sight over his right eye. His laser range finder and designator can then illuminate a target for smart missiles to attack. His helmet also incorporates a low light television camera as well as an air filter and a loud hailer system which could include a translation facility. A series of microdots implanted on the surface of his combat suit contain light-sensitive chemicals which respond to a new environment producing an ever-changing camouflage pattern. His jointed body armour extends to the groin. His boots and gloves are sealed with the rest of his suit to protect him from chemical and bacterial attack, but a fine capillary network sandwiched within the suit material contains cooling and heating fluids.

THE MAKING OF UNIFORMS

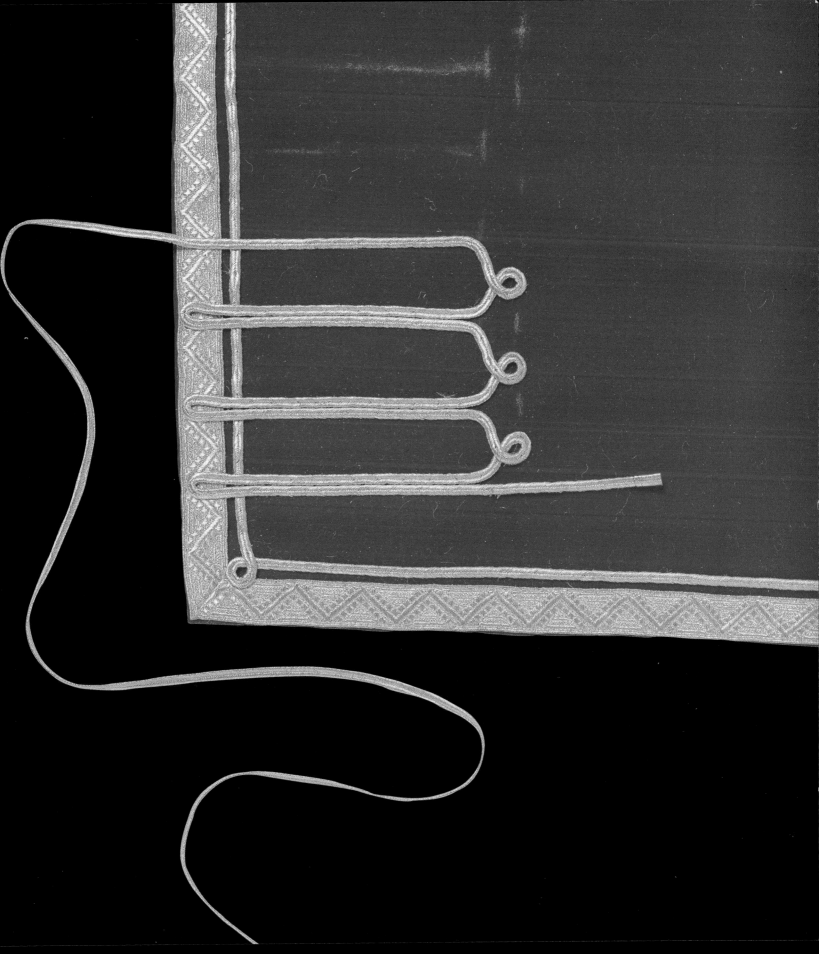

Anonymous Italian tailor painted towards the end of the 16th century by Battista Moroni. Civilian fashion was the first model for military wear in the 17th century, but by the 18th century military garments began to influence civilian clothes.

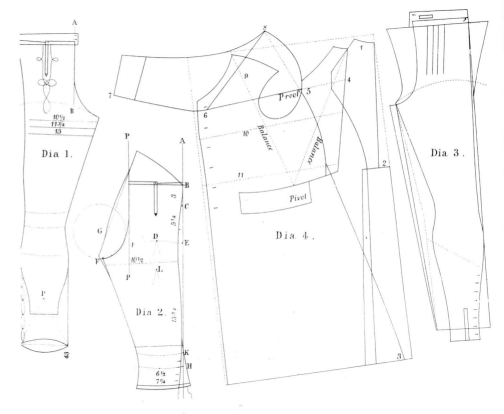

Plate of cloth cutting patterns for early 19th century trousers reproduced in Edward Giles' *The Art of Cutting* of 1887. Diagram 1 on the left shows a pattern for trousers known as Wellingtons.

UNIFORM MAKERS

The making of uniforms became an industry in the 17th century. Indeed, it was the mass-manufacturing processes established in the 17th century, arising in reponse to the greatly increased demand for military weapons and equipment in this war-torn period, that created the potential for uniformity in military clothes. An increase in the flow of capital and the creation of wealth by the end of the 17th century helped to fuel this new industry and soon there were numerous uniform manufacturers throughout Western Europe. Previous to this, the civilian clothes making industry had operated on a much smaller scale, basically thriving as an haute couture process, making clothes for individual customers of the mercantile middle class and the aristocracy. The middle class market had increased rapidly in wealth and influence in the 15th century, originating in the successful trading city states of Italy and the Low Countries. By the 16th century there was a thriving fashion industry in all Western European cities with designers from Italy, France, Germany and Spain riding various trends as the most sought after craftsmen.

In Britain, in the 17th century, it was from workshops in major cities such as London and Bristol that the first bids came for supplying various big military contracts. When the many wars of this period came to an end, these clothing manufacturers had much spare capacity and turned their attention to supplying the standing army of the British government and the various aristocrats who founded individual regiments, thus inventing a uniforms industry supplying military clothes and equipment throughout periods of war and peace. Small fortunes could be made in times of war with new recruits needing to be furnished but this would be more than offset by times of peace and reduced demand. Despite this fluctuating market, uniform manufacturers seem to have compensated for this not by diversifying into civilian wear, but by increasing the range of their military goods on offer to the principal buyers as well as supplying later quasi-military customers such as huntsmen or the police. In the 19th century, manufacturers became more aware of the global market and Peter Tait of Limerick in Ireland moved on from making clothes for the British Army during the Crimean War in the 1850s to producing uniforms for the Confederate Army in the 1860s.

Running alongside this business were the high-class tailors and craftsmen working for the civilian market who were requested by officers to make uniforms especially for them, one-off items that had the same degree of attention and materials lavished on them as any high-quality civilian fashion. Today this function is still supplied by tailors such as Gieves & Hawkes of Saville Row who create individual military clothes for officers willing to spend extra money on their attire.

In the 18th and 19th centuries, the process of clothing a soldier began when a colonel's supplier or clothier presented his patterns and budget to the General Officers of the Army's Clothing Board in Westminster. Having checked that the quality and design of this proposal conformed to the standards set, the approved patterns were sealed and the supplier made his contracts with tailors and a whole range of sub-contractors, including many unskilled workmen and women who were given simple tasks as part of the overall process of putting items of clothing together. Sometimes these people might work in separate locations, but clothing firms usually grouped them all together in one building where one could see all the tasks involved in making a uniform. Major J.W. Ferguson describes such a factory in 1861 in the United States, in Richmond, Virginia: 'Every portion of the work has its appropriate department. In the upper story of the building is the cutting room, under the direction of superintendents, and lively with the noise of shears. Lower down is the trimming room. Then the department for letting out the making of the clothes, the work being given out to the wives and relatives of the soldiers, and to poor and deserving needlewomen. Lastly comes the packing department, where the clothing, blankets, &c., are packed and forwarded to the camps.'[65]

In Britain, the finished uniforms would be checked in the warehouse by Inspectors of Clothing and then sent to army camps where they entered the control of the army quartermaster who oversaw their issue and fitting. At all stages, this process was vulnerable to corruption and a satirical work of 1787 recommends how a colonel can justify shortchanging his soldiers: 'The shorter the soldiers' coats are, the better will they be calculated for expeditious marching; and cutting them off a good deal in the skirts will not in the least increase your clothier's account, though it will give the men the more soldier like appearance... Let the sleeves also be short, that they may not obstruct the soldiers in handling their arms, and tight, that they may shew off their shape to advantage…'.[66] Frequently, the uniforms would arrive damaged or incorrectly sized and regimental tailors were employed to make good, working from dawn until sunset. The least skilled of these army tailors were nicknamed 'Dungs'.

The cross influences of civilian and military fashion have always been strong. In the 17th century, the earliest uniforms had simply been uniform versions of civilian fashion, but by the 18th century, with military influences coming from abroad, army styles were beginning to effect civilian fashion. This can be seen in some of the earliest examples of pattern books when influential tailors placed military and civilians patterns next to each other. In his *The Art of Cutting* published in 1887, Edward Giles quotes a pattern book from the beginning of the 19th century describing pantaloon trousers: 'This is one of those articles of dress, devised by fashion, and wherein the human shape is altogether unconcerned… When made with loops, or buttons, at the side [these trousers] receive another name, and are called Wellington's from the circumstances (no doubt) of their being first worn by the Military.'[67]

Elsewhere, Giles quotes from the same source describing another new style of trousers: 'Cossack Trowsers have lately been very fashionable, and although they cannot lay much claim to elegance, may yet please from their novelty. Notwithstanding the rude shapelessness of this garment, it will be necessary in measuring that you take the three principal lengths, namely, the hip, knee, and bottom; also the waistband, and that is all you need take.' These wide, shapeless trousers, apparently inspired by a visit by the Russian Czar to Britain in 1814, are also claimed as the model for the traditional flared trousers worn by sailors: 'The Sailor's Trowsers (or as called by them the gunmouth'd trowsers) are cut in the usual manner upwards; and from the crutch downwards, resemble the Cossacks, being, perhaps, yet wider at the bottom, the length of the foot being a rule for the half width; but no drawing ribband for Jack!'[68] Boots were another item inspired by military associations, as indicated by *The Whole Art of Dress by a Cavalry Officer* in 1830: 'The Hessian [named after German mercenaries] is a boot only worn with tight pantaloons, a fashion copied from the military… The Wellington, together with the following, are the only boots in general wear; to be anything like the fashion, they should have the toes at least

120

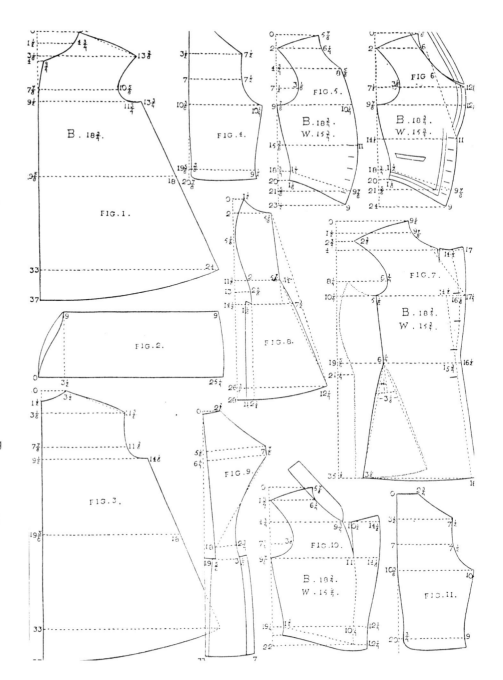

Cloth patterns from *The Gentleman's Magazine of Fashion* published in 1850, featuring in figs. 4-6 Dress waistcoats and figs. 7-9 a frock-coat. All these designs could be used for both civilian and military clothing.

an inch and half square... Bluchers [named after a Prussian general] and Collegians are a half-boot...'.[69]

Today, military uniforms continue to be made in Britain some 300 years after their invention. The more traditional ceremonial uniforms are made by a handful of companies whose histories sometimes go all the way back to the 17th century. Frequently these companies began as specialist craftsmen producing one item for the British Army and then this progressed to creating whole uniforms with all their regalia. One of the oldest established is Firmin & Sons Ltd. which can trace its beginnings back to Thomas Firmin in the City of London who won a contract to provide brass buttons for the Royal Regiment of Artillery around 1680 – up until this time, buttons had been made of silk or woven metal thread. In 1754, Nathaniel Firmin, the founder's grandson, received a Royal Warrant of Appointment to the Household of King George II to supply buttons, regalia and badges, and the company has enjoyed royal patronage ever since. They were one of the first companies to make regimental badges. Firmin can now supply an entire range of ceremonial military uniforms and equipment.

Hobson & Sons Ltd. was founded in 1850 as a maker of military caps in Woolwich but soon graduated to making uniform clothing, leather equipment and regalia. Around 1900, they left their old factory and expanded into several buildings in central London. In one building in Lexington Street in Soho one could find them making gold and silver braids, cords and fringes on steam-powered looms on one floor, hand embroidered regimental banners and colours on another, on the ground floor tailored officers' uniforms and in the basement leather belts and holsters. By the 1930s, their principal factory moved to Thundersley in Essex where it became busy making uniforms for the coming war, including tropical clothing. Since then, Hobson & Sons have consolidated around the Essex factory and continue to make a whole range of equipment and clothing for the British Ministry of Defence and armies around the world.

In recent years, the certainty of making hand-made uniforms in Britain has been undercut by foreign competition. As a result some companies have been reduced to simply operating as importers of items from around the world, but Hobson are proud to declare that they continue to manufacture all their own goods, employing over 150 people, exporting to some 80 countries, and thus keeping alive many of the traditional uniform crafts.

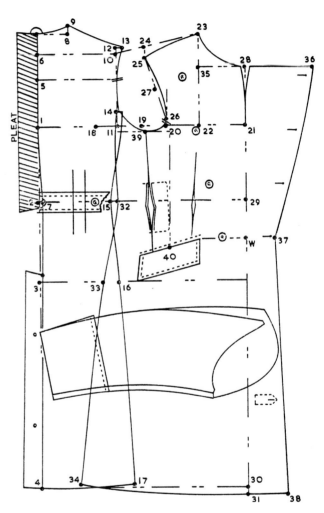

Cloth patterns for an Army Officer's Greatcoat from the *Cutter's Practical Guide* of 1955.

DYES AND COLOURS

The use of natural pigments to dye cloth has been understood in Britain since prehistory. Woad is perhaps the most well known of the naturally occurring plant dyes and this broad-leaved weed-like plant can dye plain wool tunics a variety of blues and greens. Other substances used in the ancient and medieval period include madder root (red), oak tannin and walnut husks (dark brown), onion skins (yellow or brown), greenweed and the flowerheads of reeds (green), elder bark and meadowsweet (black). By the 17th century, the clothing industry had grown to such an extent that additional quantities of dyes were being imported from Europe and the newly acquired colonies of the Caribbean. Large quantities of madder came from Amsterdam via Bristol and equally large amounts of indigo entered Bristol from the West Indies. This, in addition to locally produced dyes, meant that in the West Country alone, tens of thousands of jackets every year could be dyed either red or blue. These two colours remained the first choice for military clothing as their process of dyeing consisted of just one stage, whereas other colours could only be achieved on any scale by double dyeing, which meant not only more time but more costly ingredients. For example, green could be achieved by dyeing first blue then yellow, while orange was first red and then yellow, purple being created from blue then red. An alternative to dyeing was, of course, just to use the natural colour of wool and both grey and a bleached white were popular alternatives for uniform colours when a military budget was tight.

The traditional process of dyeing begins with the cloth itself. A raw fleece is first cleaned with human urine to remove any grease or dirt. This is one of several processes in which human urine features as a vital ingredient and in the past urine would never be thrown away but stored in buckets at home and in public places such as pubs where it would be sold to the urine collector, sometimes known as 'Piss Harry', who would then make a comfortable living out of it selling it on to cloth manufacturers. William Partridge in his *Practical Treatise on Dyeing* in 1823 describes its qualities: 'Urine that is fresh voided will not scour well. That from persons on a plain diet is stronger and better than that from luxurious livers. The cider and gin drinkers are considered to give the worst, the beer drinkers the best. When urine is collected it should be kept in close vessels until it has completely undergone those changes by which ammonia is developed.'[70] After cleaning, the raw wool was then carded, that is, the fibres brushed to remove tangles in readiness for the process of spinning and weaving into cloth.

Raw cloth was taken to a dyeing house where it would be soaked in water and fuller's earth, a highly absorbent clay used to absorb more grease from the cloth. With washing, shrinking and beating or pressing, the cloth would increase in weight and bulk, become 'fuller', and was now ready for dyeing. A recipe for dyeing 60lbs of wool scarlet, recorded in Partridge's treatise of 1823, lists: '1lb cochineal [powdered American insect], 3lbs madder, 6lbs argol [deposit from fermented wine], 3lbs alum [metal sulphate used as a mordant to fix the colour], 4 pints tin liquor [derived from tin, a mordant used especially for creating scarlet] 6lbs cutbear [rock lichen found by the sea], and two buckets of urine.' The alum, argol and tin liquor were boiled together in a vat for half an hour, then the madder and cochineal added for a further ten minutes. The wool was now added and boiled for two hours in this liquid, which was then run off and the wool cleaned. A fresh liquid was made of 6lbs of cutbear and two buckets of urine and the wool plunged into this for another two hours. Dyed and cleaned, scarlet cloth was stretched over tenter racks and left to dry outside. It was then combed with teasels, originally the bristly head of a flower, to create a nap, a soft fuzzy texture, on the cloth. Tightly rolled, the cloth was finally immersed in hot water to give it a permanent lustre. Thus was recreated the scarlet cloth of the British redcoat.

A traditional centre for cloth making in Britain was Gloucestershire where wool had been produced from Cotswold sheep since the Middle Ages, with the town of Stroud becoming a centre for dyeing. The water of Stroud was believed to contain special ingredients enabling the production of the finest scarlet cloth and though this was more due to the skills of its dyers, Stroudwater scarlet became famous and dyed textiles made in Stroud were sold around the world. An old joke had it that news of a rainy day in Moscow would create drunkeness in Stroud as the pristine white jackets of the Czar's soldiers would need to be replaced, thus guaranteeing weeks of extra work and wages.

Today, camouflage fabric is the main material of military uniforms and Strines Textiles is one of its leading producers. For 200 years, Strines has been located in the same part of

Cheshire, near Stockport, where a lake provides all the water needed for the process of dyeing. Each year, it produces some two million metres of camouflage fabric, most of it for the British Army, but also for several other countries, including the armies of Belgium, Germany, Australia, U.S.A., Sweden, the Netherlands, Denmark, Kuwait, France, Thailand, Malaysia and South Africa. The process of creating camouflage fabric begins with the receipt of plain fabric from suppliers. For Ministry of Defence contracts, each roll of fabric is stamped with a number so that each stage of manufacture can be traced in order to maintain quality control. The plain fabric is sewn together to form a belt of material and is cleaned to remove any size from the cloth. If the fabric is synthetic, it is heated to stabilise it at the required width.

The standard pattern for British Disruptive Pattern Material is received from the Ministry of Defence as a sealed sample of one square metre, just as sealed samples have been supplied for 200 years to all uniform contractors. The different motif layers of the camouflage pattern are separated and traced onto celluloid film. This film is then wrapped around a lacquer-coated rotary screen of 100 per cent nickel imported from Holland. The pattern can be scanned directly onto the screens with a laser, but at Strines the process is carried out by ultra-violet light exposure which penetrates the clear parts of the celluloid film,

leaving the motif covered parts of the lacquer untouched. Rotary screens now bearing each motif layer of the pattern are ready to be fitted to the print machine. In the meantime, dyes are mixed in the colour shop according to a computerised recipe based on the Ministry of Defence standard. Various weights of colour are added, as well as penetrating and thickening agents. Carbon black is added for its infrared qualities. Acid colours are used for nylon, Disperse colours for polyester, Vat colours for cotton, and Basic colours for acrylic.

Plain fabric is fed into the print machine on a print blanket. Five rollers are used on the machine. The first roller has a sticky surface which picks up any fluff or pieces of dirt that have contaminated the fabric. The other four rollers are the four rotary screens, each printing one motif layer of the final camouflage pattern. The four camouflage dyes – green, khaki, brown and black – are poured into each of the rotary screens. Once the pattern has been printed on the fabric, it passes through a drying oven. Out of the print machine, the fabric is moved to a steaming machine. Here, steam heat sets off a chemical reaction which fixes the dyes in the fabric. A washer machine removes any unfixed dye and the fabric is dried. Finally, a stenter machine stretches the fabric to its required width.

To meet the high requirements of the Ministry of Defence, the printed fabric is thoroughly inspected and tested in a

Colour shop at Strines Textiles where dyes are mixed according to computerised recipes to produce the colours for British Disruptive Pattern camouflage according to Ministry of Defence specifications.

British Disruptive Pattern camouflage motifs traced onto celluloid films which are then wrapped around nickel rotary screens and exposed to ultra-violet light. This light reacts with the light sensitive lacquer on the screens to create patterns ready for printing.

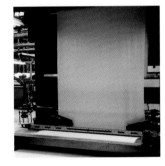

Plain fabric being fed into the printing machine.

Gaps between the rotary screens on the printing machine reveal the camouflage fabric freshly printed.

The removal of a faulty rotary screen on the printing machine provides an opportunity to see the camouflage pattern being built up from several layers of shapes and colours.

laboratory to ensure it possesses all its required qualities. A certificate is issued at the end of the process. Such meticulous concern for its performance means camouflage fabric does not come cheap and costs considerably more than printed fabric for the fashion industry. Any camouflage fabric used for fashion clothes has usually been produced to a far lower standard. The British DPM pattern is not copyrighted, whereas most other major patterns, such as those used by the U.S. and German armies, are protected and their nations retain the legal powers to intervene if they feel the camouflage pattern is being misused.

JACKETS AND TROUSERS

The making of military uniform tunics, jackets and trousers is a relatively simple affair with the basic process unchanged for several hundred years. Sewing machines and computerised cutting machines have increased the rate of work, but much of the procedure is still reliant on hand finishing and attention to detail with constant inspections. The process begins with cutting the material. Traditionally in tailoring the client is measured and these measurements are transferred to paper, cloth or card templates which are then laid on the chosen cloth, marked and cut with scissors. Standard patterns were created for military uniforms and kept by uniform manufacturers. Sometimes they were published in pattern books. Today such information is stored on computers and can be called up on cutting machines which automatically cut the required shape material. Once the cutting has taken place, the individual pieces of cloth have an interlining or fusible attached to them to make them thicker and keep their shape. They are then machined together and the item is assembled, with additions such as button-holes and further lining made at this stage. Pressing gives the item shape as well as the required creases. Any ornamentation, such as braiding or buttons, is hand sewn.

Hand cutting cloth using a cardboard template.

Finishing a pair of trousers by hand, showing buttons and lining.

Pressing a pair of trousers to give it shape and the required creases.

Attaching gold cord by hand to a jacket.

Finished jacket for the Royal Horse Artillery waits on a hanger at Hobson & Sons Ltd.

RECREATING A COLDSTREAM GUARDS JACKET *c.*1815

This process begins with drafting a pattern based on looking at original uniforms from the period to be reconstructed. Examples of Napoleonic uniforms can be found in some national museums and a pattern can be based on these. The basic measurements of the client are then taken and a toile is cut out of calico or cheap cotton, that is, roughly approximate cloth shapes which are then placed on the client for the first fitting, being marked with chalk to show alteration lines. Having secured the correct measurements and shapes, these are cut into the fabric, which for an ordinary soldier is red wool. Traditional scarlet wool can be bought today from Abimelech Hainsworth who supply it to the British Army, but it is much lighter than it would have been in the Napoleonic era when cloth of at least double the thickness would have given a uniform a certain stoutness. Once the body of the uniform is cut out, this is then mounted with a layer of linen which is 'pad-stitched' to give it shape. Each piece of the body is now stitched together along agreed seam lines. With the body of the uniform assembled, minus its arms and collar, a second fitting is made with the client. Here, the arm holes are calculated and the sleeves can be made. At this stage, lacing is attached, the means by which British Napoleonic regiments were identified, and is made out of white worsted stitched on

with linen thread. The skirt pieces of the jacket which were turned back to show the lining are made with an inner lining of lambswool serge and an outer lining of white wool. The rest of the body is lined with just the lambswool serge. After a final fitting, the sleeves are attached to the body. Button holes are cut and stitched. Buttons are sewn on, either just plain pewter or replicas of moulded buttons with engraved regimental designs on them.

A toile is cut and marked with chalk in the first stage of reconstructing the Guards jacket.

Cut pieces of the jacket lined with linen and with the gold thread used for the lacing on the front.

Second fitting of the jacket on the client. At this stage, the arm holes are calculated and the sleeves made up of calico.

Cutting and tailoring have created a strong sense of shape for the back of the jacket.

LEATHERWORK

Before the advent of webbing in the 20th century, all soldiers' equipment straps and belts were made of leather. Pouches and boxes for carrying equipment were also made out of leather. The making of leather equipment was an industry all on its own, although bigger military suppliers included it alongside their other crafts. To make a leather pouch box of the sort carried by a Hussar in the early 19th century, a traditional procedure would be followed. Standard shapes were chalked on and cut out of bridle leather, vegetable or oak tanned, supplied as backs or sides of a cow. Stitching lines were marked on the shapes and scored with a divider-like implement. A pricking iron, like a fork, was tapped lightly onto these lines, creating a series of holes. A stitching awl, a thick diamond-shaped needle, pierces these holes, making them diagonal for pieces fixed at right angles or straight for two pieces on top of each other.

Waxed linen thread is placed through two saddler's needles, one at each end of the thread. With the pieces of leather clamped on a block to keep them in shape, or held in a wooden saddler's clam, the two needles are now used to stitch the leather together, using the holes already pierced for the needles. Once assembled, the leather box is then shaved at the edges, the edges being dyed with black ink and burnished with canvas or a stick. This helps to flatten the grain, making the edge tougher and less likely to peel or dent. The finished leather pouch is ready to be polished. This can be achieved by burnishing with a wooden rod, applying a mixture of wax and oil, and rubbing with a cloth. Patenting, a very high gloss, is achieved with layers of black lacquer painted and sanded between coats.

Reconstructed Hussar Pouch Box c.1830. Such an exquisite, but ultimately tiny container, would have been used to hold money and personal belongings.

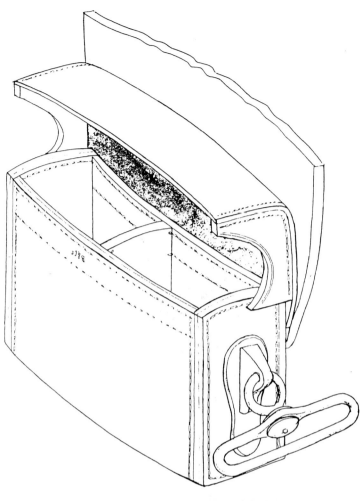

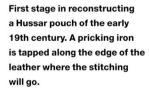

Line drawing of a Royal Artillery Pouch of 1862 now in the National Army Museum, drawn by Pierre Turner. Such research is the basis on which historically authentic reconstructions can be made today.

First stage in reconstructing a Hussar pouch of the early 19th century. A pricking iron is tapped along the edge of the leather where the stitching will go.

An awl is used to pierce the holes marked by the pricking iron. The two pieces of leather to be joined are held in a wooden saddler's clam held between the knees of the leatherworker.

Using two saddler's needles with waxed thread, the pouch box is stitched together.

A wooden stick is used to burnish the stitched edges of the pouch box, making them tougher and more resistant to wear.

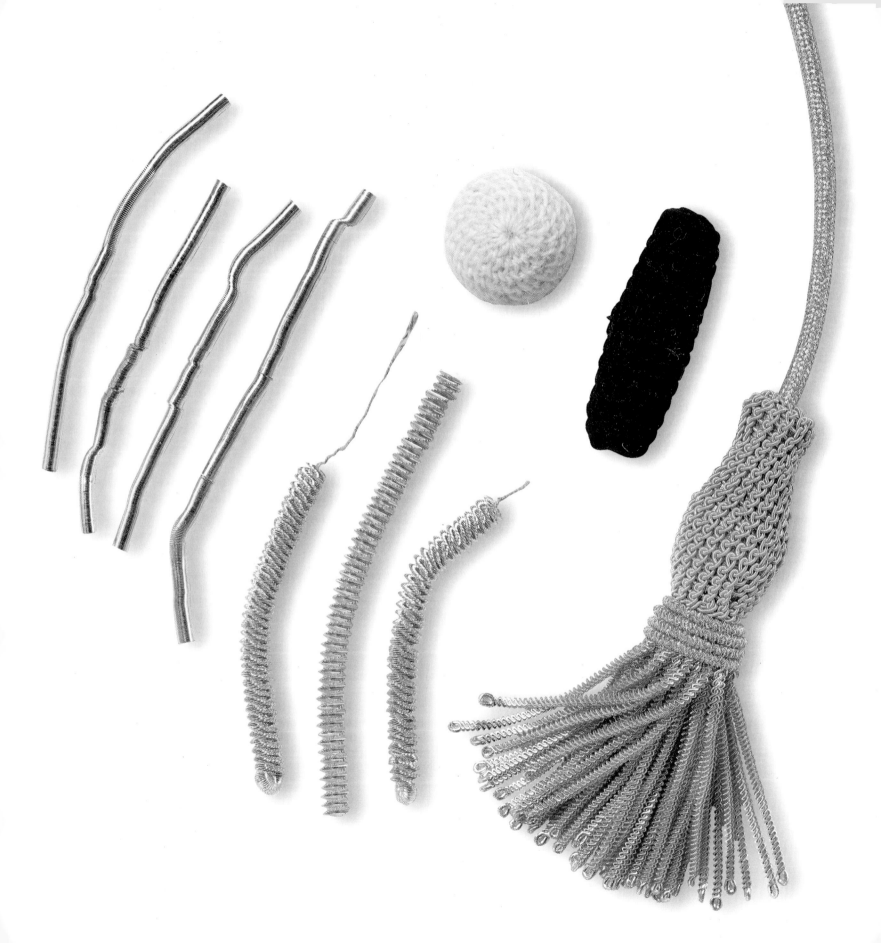

TASSELS AND GOLD

One of the most spectacular aspects of military ceremony is the array of gold regalia fixed to soldiers' uniforms. Not surprisingly this is the most expensive dimension of uniform manufacture both in materials and in time. When a simple badge made out of gold purl can take four hours to sew, then the cost of more elaborate items can be fully appreciated. In the 19th century, the gold cord worn on a Hussar's jacket might actually be made of solid gold wire, but today thick gold cord usually has a core of cotton around which a golden thread is wound.

A gold tassel, however, is still a complex achievement in miniature, requiring the finest gold cord and delicate craftsmanship. Pure gold for this work is supplied in the form of gold purl, that is, gold in the form of a tiny, fine spring. This can either be cut into tiny hollow sections which are then pulled onto a gold thread for sewing a badge or, in the case of a tassel, a copper wire is twisted with silk and then placed inside the gold purl which is spun around it with the aid of a small drill to create the fine gold cord. A round wooden mould is wound with silk and the fine lengths of gold cord sewn to it. Such a process takes hours of intense concentration and is still carried out by hand.

Gold cord twisted into an ornamental knot.

Opposite, materials used in creating a gold tassel. From left to right: pure gold purl; gold purl that has been spun round a wire to create gold cord; cotton and wood moulds to which gold thread is attached; the finished gold tassel.

Gold cord attached to a recreated officer's epaulette worn on the shoulder of the jacket.

Gold cord being spun ready for attaching to a tassel.

Simple wooden mould of a tassel being covered in gold thread.

Badge being sewn with gold purl on gold thread.

MILITARY HATS

Military uniform hats, including caps, busbies and bearskins, continue to be made in a way that has changed little over the last 100 years, emphasising the close involvement of individual craftspeople in their manufacture.

Military caps begin their life as a series of shaped pieces of cloth cut in accordance to standard patterns or bevels. These pieces, plus the crown, piping, and lining, are machined together. Having created the basic cap shape, eyelets (ventilation holes) are inserted, between two and four per cap, and then this is hand pressed to give it shape. Stiffeners are glued, then machined inside the cap, and finally the peak, head leather, badges and any other particular attributes are attached by hand to the cap. A busby, a smaller version of the bearskin, is made of arctic fox fur dyed black for an officer or of artificial fur for other ranks. The fur is stretched, then cut and handsewn into the basic shape. This is then stretched over the body of the hat which has a leather top and brow. Finally, it is trimmed.

Feathers and plumes for ceremonial hats and helmets require a separate skill which is usually undertaken by a specialist craftsmen such as Louis Chalmers of the Plumery. Household Cavalry plumes are made of Mongolian horse hair gathered humanely by herders who first trim the tails of their horses to remove the split ends and the follow-

Mongolian horse hair dyed red, on the left, for making the plumes of the Blues and Royals, Royal Household Cavalry. Section of fur used to make bearskin caps worn by the Foot Guards.

Standard metal pattern shapes or bevels for a military peaked cap arranged on a cutting machine.

Soft cut pieces are machined together to form basic cap shapes.

ing season cut a larger section from the tails to be sent abroad. This horse hair is then either bleached white or dyed red or black, woven and fixed on to a metal stem which is then inserted into the spike of the cavalry helmets. Officer's plumes are made from yak hair from Tibet. A small scandal was recently created when a military attaché in Peking was presented with the hair from 50 yaks shot dead to provide plumes for Blues and Royals officers. When they were returned to Britain, the plume manufacturer was outraged, not only was there no need to kill the yaks, it could simply have been cut off, but the black yak hair was the wrong colour – it was impossible to dye and full of maggots.

The skills that go into the making of horsehair plumes are at least 2,000 years old and for the reconstruction of an ancient Roman helmet, the vertical plume worn by a Grenadier guard was simply adapted to a horizontal shape where it was handsewn and slipped into a crest box of brass attached to the helmet. A variety of feathers were worn in 19th century hats which are now no longer available, but many natural substitutes are possible. A Hussar's plume that would originally have been made from white egret and red vulture feathers mounted on whalebone, is now made from burnt white ostrich and cut red maribu feathers mounted on blackened aluminium. Swan feathers, used most spectacularly in generals' hats, are today gath-

ered humanely from the Abbotsbury Swannery. Dyed goose or turkey hackle feathers are now the most widely used in military plumes and these are attached by hand with hemp to a stem.

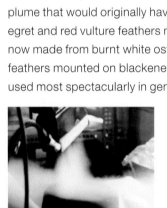

Stiffened cap is shaped on a block with a steam iron.

Finished cap is stretched on a five-piece wooden block.

Arctic fox fur is cut to shape of the busby body next to it.

Finished busby waiting to be trimmed.

Red dyed Mongolian horsehair attached to the stem ready for insertion into a cavalry helmet. Bleached and natural horsehair, humanely gathered, beneath it.

RECREATING A NAPOLEONIC SHAKO

The recreation of a Belgic shako of the type worn by a British Foot Guards Officer at the battle of Waterloo in 1815 begins with a rough cone of felt. The felt is dipped into hot water and attached with cord to a wooden hat block to dry. Once dry, the felt is shellacked, that is, painted with a varnish mixture of resin and methylated spirit to stiffen it. Several pieces of stiffened felt are stitched together, along with a leather peak and neck flap and a hessian lining for inside the hat (for an officer this would originally have been silk). Finally, the regimental badge, rosette, plume and gold cord are stitched to the finished hat.

Dipped in hot water, the basic felt cone is pulled onto a hat block to dry.

Opposite, ostrich feather plume, on left, and sample plume made of a variety of dyed feathers.

The dried felt hat is shellacked to stiffen it.

The various pieces of stiffened felt and leather are sewn together.

Dyed goose feathers are tied to a stem to make a plume.

The finished Belgic shako of the type worn at the battle of Waterloo in 1815.

SPIT AND POLISH

The Life Guards are the premier regiment of the British Army, taking precedence over all others, and it is no surprise to learn that it is they who are the leading experts in 'spit and polish', the techniques of keeping their uniform and equipment clean. As members of the Household Cavalry Mounted Regiment, alongside elements from the Blues and Royals, they are the soldiers in glittering breastplates and helmets with plumes who parade alongside Her Majesty the Queen on ceremonial occasions. They can also be seen every day patiently guarding the Horse Guards building in Whitehall surrounded by thousands of tourists from around the world wanting their photograph taken in front of them. As showcase warriors, their uniform and equipment must be of the very highest standard and it is to them that other regiments of the British Army come for advice on cleaning and maintenance.

Competition is keen for the cleanest, most perfect outfit within the Household Cavalry with the leading troopers of the Life Guards and the Blues and Royals battling it out in teams of six every year to win the Richmond Cup, presented by the Queen for the best turned out troop. Further incentive is provided by the fact that every unit sent on parade is first inspected thoroughly to ensure perfection – those who fail to pass the test spend the rest of the day on foot, standing and marching in their uncomfortable riding boots, while those who are cleanest get to sit on their horses all day in the covered sentry boxes. Any trooper who continually shows a lack of application to 'spit and polish' is removed from parade duty and ends up in the kitchen doing menial tasks. The process of cleaning uniform and equipment in readiness for parade can take the whole of the previous day and sometimes the previous night as well. One trooper, determined to be the smartest soldier in the British Army spent the whole day cleaning and polishing, took a one hour break in the pub, and then continued to work solidly throughout the night without sleep to ensure that on the morning of parade, his outfit was perfect.

A typical day of cleaning kit in the Life Guards begins with the trooper's horse. An afternoon, from 2.00pm to 5.00pm, is spent cleaning the horse's equipment, including the sheepksin saddle and its white leather straps. Four and a half hours from 5.30pm is then devoted to the soldier's uniform, although this can take much longer, depending on the deter-

Dismounted Life Guard faces the gaze of tourists while on duty at Horse Guards in Whitehall in central London. These troops, among the smartest in the world, escort Her Majesty the Queen on ceremonial occasions.

mination of the individual trooper – waking up at 3.00am the following morning is a common occurrence just to make sure the soldier's boots are returned to the gleaming polish which may have faded in the intervening hours, just in time for morning inspection.

The 'whites' are the first pieces of kit to be cleaned, these include the white leather gauntlets, belts, buckskins and sword straps. They are scrubbed vigorously to remove any of the old white covering and taken back to the bare buff. Sometimes when the leather has become worn smooth, a file is used to roughen it up. A white pigment mixed with water, not a paint, called 'white sap' is dabbed on to the leather with a sponge until every section on display is covered. On pieces of leather that rub against buckles and thus frequently break their white covering, the typewriting eraser fluid Tippex is used for extra fine coverage. In a special display of attention to detail, the stitching on the belts and straps is picked out using a pencil point to remove the white sap from the tiny holes and thus create a greater sense of 'definition', which is one of the chief concepts behind judging the perfection of 'spit and polish'. The master saddler, 'however' is known to frown upon this piece of bravura display as the pencil point weakens the leatherwear and so a truly politic trooper will always check which officers will be inspecting him the next morning and design his cleaning regime according to individual tastes and prejudices.

The great knee-high riding boots worn by the Life Guards are the next item to be cleaned. Kept on metre-long wooden shoe trees which help the trooper to clean them without touching them, they are first prepared for polishing by having beeswax melted into them, thus making them as stiff as board, excess beeswax being removed with the back of a polish tin. Attention is then given to any creases caused by wear. These must be removed completely, literally disappearing into a glass-like sheen through 'tinning in', using the edge of the polish tin to smooth the wax into the rough leather, and then brushing off any excess. The work of polishing can now begin, called 'padding out'. A 'didge' is worn over the first two fingers, comprised of a very soft cloth attached to an old pair of tights which are tied around the wrist and arm. The 'didge' is dabbed in water and then dabbed in Kiwi black polish, the British Army's standard boot polish. The polish is massaged into the creases first and then applied to the rest of the boots. With the polish worked into the leather, barely any polish is applied to the 'didge' and the process of 'bobbing' begins which brings out the glass-like sheen of the finished boots. Each boot can take approximately two hours to polish. In pursuit of the holy grail of 'definition', white sap is applied to the inside leather of the boots and a black marker pen used to highlight the line where the rough white leather meets the polished black leather. Finally, the metal heelplate is cleaned

The 'whites' are the first items of the Life Guard uniform to be cleaned. Having had their old white surface removed, the gauntlets are being coated with 'white sap', a mixture of white pigment and water.

The secret to being the smartest Life Guard on parade is 'definition', showing off the line between white and black on equipment. Here, a trooper uses a black marker pen to highlight the edge on the inside of his boot.

An extra smart aspect of preparing gauntlets for parade is to mark each stitch on the leather with pencil, although some officers frown on this as it wears out the leather.

A brush (or back of a tin) is used to smooth out creases on a boot which could have been worn on parade for decades.

A 'didge' is used to apply polish to the boot and gentle polishing for up to an hour creates a glass-like effect on the leather.

with wire wool and a silver pen used to highlight the line where it meets the black leather. With such painstaking maintenance, these boots can last for years and are passed on from trooper to trooper.

A Life Guard's 'brasses' include the brass and metal cuirass, or breast and back plates, supporting straps, and the helmet with plume holder. For cleaning, the armour is stripped down to its various elements. Cotton wool is dabbed into Brasso, the standard British Army metal cleaning fluid, and rubbed into the equipment. Excess Brasso is wiped off and polishing begins, but on complex items such as crests and roses where the detail in the metalwork retains bits of Brasso, chalk dust is dabbed onto them and then brushed off, thus removing the excess. On the smooth surfaces of the breastplate or the helmet, no brushing is allowed to scratch the surface and bare fingers are used to rub the polish into the metal. Even the inside back of the helmet is polished as this can be inspected in the reflection of the back plate. A black marker pen is used again to highlight the 'definition' between the inside black leather lining of the cuirass and the outside metal.

The horsehair plume worn on the top of the metal helmet is washed in water like hair with shampoo. In order to keep the hairs of the plume hanging straight down, the plume is placed inside a piece of cloth tubing, tied with string to keep the shape of the 'onion' at the top of the plume, and then

sprayed with hairspray and left overnight on a radiator, only being unwrapped at the very last moment. The red tunic worn by the Life Guards is simply brushed to keep it clean or drycleaned when necessary. A trooper will usually have two such tunics, one for wearing beneath armour which receives marks from the metal, and one for wearing without armour. When all these stages of cleaning and maintenance are completed, the individual trooper is ready to face the inspection of his officers and the attention of thousands of tourists. Taking a day and possibly a night of work, it is little wonder the Life Guards are the elite unit of the British Army when it comes to 'spit and polish'.

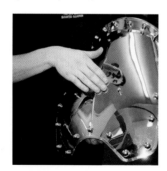

Chalk dust is brushed gently off the helmet to remove any remaining polish from the metal.

Bare fingers are used to apply the metal polish on the smooth face of the cuirass.

The horsehair plume is brushed before being fixed to the helmet.

The plume is placed inside a material stocking and then tied at the top to form the 'onion'. Coated with hairspray, the plume is then placed on a radiator overnight and only removed at the last moment.

Locker of a Life Guard trooper showing all of his kit which has to be cleaned before parade. The 'cricket-bat' shoe trees in the boots are useful handles when polishing them. Two scarlet jackets are issued to each trooper, one to be worn under armour which gets marked by the metal, and one to be worn without the cuirass.

**Spit and polish 100 years ago.
British Army company barrack
room of 1896, all kit has been
meticulously cleaned and
presented ready for inspection.**

ENTERTAINMENT

Angels and Bermans of London are the biggest entertainment costumiers in the world, supplying productions in theatre, television and cinema with the finest recreated clothes from all periods. Their work has appeared in some of the greatest movies of all time, including films in which the costume designer has won an Oscar, such as *Cleopatra* in 1963, *Barry Lyndon* in 1975, *The Last Emperor* in 1988 and *Bram Stoker's Dracula* in 1993. An important aspect of their service is the providing of accurate historical uniforms. In Stephen Spielberg's 1998 movie *Saving Private Ryan*, hundreds of World War Two uniforms are required and Angels and Bermans have to get it exactly right. Specialist military advisers are called on, but Angels also have their own remarkable research resources including an extensive library of literary sources and what is known as the Badge Room, a massive room containing over 4,500 samples of military, naval, and airforce badges, regalia, armbands, and uniforms, many of them original examples collected over the last 50 years. The Badge Room is, in effect, a vast private museum, and Gerald Moulin, a senior member of Angels is still collecting now. Recently, he arrived in Moscow with 70,000 dollars in cash contained in an elaborate body belt made at Angels in order to make a deal with Russian contacts. 'I feared for my life,' he recalls, 'only days before a British businessman had been murdered by the Russian mafia.' In return for this money, Gerald managed to buy a wealth of Russian and Soviet military uniforms and equipment which will serve as the basis for any future James Bond-style Cold War movies.

Many film directors demand the very finest quality uniforms for their leading actors as they believe only true materials, such as real armour or real brass helmets, will give them that authentic period feel, but this has to be balanced with the demands of a tight budget. Angels and Bermans tread a fine line between creating a few high quality reproductions –'button-perfect' is their description – using authentic materials and designs, alongside visually effective but cheaper alternatives for uniforms worn by extras or stuntmen. 'In military films,' says Gerald Moulin, 'stuntmen can get through so many uniforms in just one scene that it would not be sensible to lavish work and materials on them.' Cotton versions of uniforms are made and armour and helmets are produced out of vacuum formed plastic, but the very best uniforms are made to last, for after filming the uniforms will be returned to Angels who can then use them again in future productions. Indeed, many of these uniforms can be hired for fancy dress parties and are expected to have a long life. Walking along the racks and shelves of equipment in their Camden headquarters is like walking through a history of warfare as well as a history of movie-making: medieval mail and plate armour from *Braveheart* is followed by buff coats and cuirasses from *Cromwell*, with 18th century naval uniforms from *Hornblower* and Napoleonic redcoats from *Sharpe* followed by World War Two German camouflage jackets for the latest Spielberg epic.

As a company, Angels and Bermans has a complex history which mirrors that of more conventional tailors over the last 200 years. Bermans and Nathans was the original form of the company, with Nathans being able to trace its history back to 1790 when it became quickly associated with the theatre. Morris Berman was a master tailor to the Czar before the family had to flee to Britain during the Russian Revolution. In Britain, his son Max made uniforms for the British Army and in World War Two many of these were used in films made by the government, but the association with film-making had already been forged with costumes created for productions by Gaumont and Gainsborough Films as well as war films of the interwar period such as *Somme* and *Arras*. Max's son, Monty Berman, served in the RAF and later became deputy managing director of the much expanded company. Angels began as a second hand clothes shop in 1840, but in the early 20th century developed into a tailor of military uniforms as well as clothes for actors. In the 1990s Angels and Bermans merged to form their leading association, with each year adding more and more uniforms and clothes to their stocks so that their current 120,00 square feet of storage in Camden will have to be enlarged even further by the beginning of the 21st century.

Opposite, Sean Bean as Sharpe, the British hero of the Bernard Cornwell novels set in the Napoleonic Wars, turned into a popular television series by Carlton. Bean wears a uniform made by Angels and Bermans based on the uniform of the 95th Rifle Regiment. The choice of a green uniform reinforces Sharpe's independent character, a soldier on the fringe of the military establishment, echoing earlier rebel heroes such as Robin Hood.

NOTES

All references to quotations only.

1: Tincey, J., *The British Army 1660-1704*, London, 1994, p.19.

2: Tincey, *ibidem*, p.39.

3: Wood, J.B., *The King's Army*, Cambridge, 1996, p.165.

4: Parker, G., *The Military Revolution*, Cambridge, 1996, p.151.

5: Elliot-Wright, P.J.C., *English Civil War*, London, 1997, p.62.

6: Gentles, I., *The New Model Army*, Oxford, 1992, p.41.

7: Eltis, D., *The Military Revolution in Sixteenth Century Europe*, London, 1995, p.60.

8: Machiavelli, N., (trans. Bernard Crick), *The Discourses*, Harmondsworth, 1970, p.504.

9: Tincey, *op.cit*., p.17.

10: Lawson, C.C.P., *A History of the Uniforms of the British Army*, London, 1940, p.46.

11: Chandler, D., *The Art of Warfare in the Age of Marlborough*, London, 1990, p.90.

12: Robertson, J.P., *Personal Adventures and Anecdotes of an Old Officer*, London, 1906, p.51.

13: Strachan, H., *British Military Uniforms 1768-1796*, London, 1975, p.145.

14: Strachan, *ibidem*, p.29.

15: Childs, J., *Armies and Warfare in Europe*, Manchester, 1982, p.200.

16: Elliot-Wright, *op.cit*., p.86.

17: Tincey, *op.cit*., p.39.

18: Tincey, *ibidem*, p.19.

19: Prestwich, M., *Armies and Warfare in the Middle Ages*, New Haven, 1996, p.141.

20: Fosten, B., and Carman, Y., *Uniforms of the Foot Guards*, Romford, 1995, p.32.

21: Haythornthwaite, P.J., 'The First Highland Regiment', *Military Illlustrated* 10, London, 1988, p.27.

22: Colley, L., *Britons*, London, 1994, p.103.

23: *The Turkish Letters of Ogier Ghiselin de Busbecq* (trans. E.S. Forster), Oxford, 1927, p.231.

24: *For King and Country: The Letters and Diaries of John Mills* (edited by I. Fletcher), Staplehurst, 1995, p.271.

25: Haythornthwaite, P., *British Cavalryman 1792-1815*, London, 1994, p.21.

26: Brzezinski, R., 'The Wings of the Polish Hussars', *Military Illustrated* 88, London, 1995, p.34.

27: Parker, *op.cit*., p.149.

28: Austen, J., *Pride and Prejudice*, Harmondsworth, 1972, pp.115-116.

29: Colley, *op.cit*., p.186.

80: *Advice to the Officers of the British Army*, London, 1787, pp.69-71.

31: Haythornthwaite, P.J., *The Armies of Wellington*, London, 1994, p.83.

32: Haythornthwaite, *ibidem*, p.83.

33: Fletcher, I., *Napoleonic Wars: Wellington's Army*, London, 1996, pp.70-72.

34: Fletcher, *ibidem*, p.69.

35: Kochan, J.L., 'Made in France: The Lottery Uniforms of the Continental Army 1777-1780', unpublished article, p.1.

36: Kochan, *ibidem*, p.7.

37: Field, R., *Mexican-American War 1846-48*, London, 1997, p.25.

38: Field, *ibidem*, p.29.

39: Field, *ibidem*, p.48.

40: Field, R., *American Civil War: Confederate Army*, London, 1996, p.128.

41: Newark, P., 'Custer's Demand', *Military Illustrated* 92, London, 1996, p.27.

42: Newark, *ibidem*, p.28.

43: Strachan, H.F.A., 'The Origin of the 1855 Uniform Changes – an Example of Pre-Crimean Reform', *Journal of the Society of Army Historical Research* 55, London, 1977, p.85.

44: Strachan, *ibidem*, p.87.

45: Barthorp, M., 'Infantry Undress Uniform 1822-1902', *Journal of the Society of Army Historical Research* 56, London, 1978, p29.

46: Strachan, H.F.A., *op.cit*., p.89.

47: Strachan, *ibidem*, p.90.

48: Tylden, G., 'The Accoutrements of the British Infantryman 1640 to 1940', *Journal of the Society of Army Historical Research* 57, London 1979, p.11.

49: Parker, *op.cit*., p.135.

50: *Tigers Round the Throne*, Zamana Gallery, London, 1990, p.26.

51: Smith, R., *American Civil War: Union Army*, London, 1996, p.12.

52: Rickwood, G.O., 'Notes and Documents', *Journal of the Society of Army Historical Research* 44, London, 1966, p.126.

53: Newark, T., Newark, Q., and Borsarello, J.F., *Brassey's Book of Camouflage*, London, 1996, p.13.

54: Newark, *ibidem*, p.14.

55: Barthorp, M., 'Notes and Documents', *Journal of the Society of Army Historical Research* 61, London, 1983, p.55.

56: *Hitler's Table-Talk* (trans. by N. Cameron and R.H. Stevens), Oxford, 1988, p.404.

57: *Hitler's Table-Talk*, *ibidem*, p.266.

58: Marley, D.F., *Pirates*, London, 1995, p.98.

59: Fischer, K.P., *Nazi Germany*, London, 1995, p.130.

60: *Hitler's Table-Talk, op.cit*., p.629.

61: *Hitler's Table-Talk, ibidem*, p.318.

62: Field, *American Civil War, op.cit.*, p.55.

63: Smith, R., *American Civil War Zouaves*, London, 1996, p.54.

64: Slavin, T., 'Now that's really smart gear', *The Observer*, London, 16th February, 1997.

65: Field, *American Civil War, op.cit*., p.118.

66: *Advice to the Officers..., op.cit*., pp.31-32.

67: Giles, E.B., *The Art of Cutting and History of English Costume*, London, 1896, p.128.

68: Giles, *ibidem*, p.129.

69: Waugh, N., *The Cut of Men's Clothes 1600-1900*, London, 1964, p.153.

70: Edwards, E.H., 'Making the Redcoat: British Army Uniform Manufacture', *Military Illustrated* 81, London, 1995, p.15.

BIBLIOGRAPHY

Abbreviations:
BHU = Brassey's History of Uniforms
JSAHR = Journal of the Society of Army Historical Research
MI = Military Illustrated
OMAA = Osprey Men-At-Arms

General works:

Carman, W.Y., *British Military Uniforms from Contemporary Pictures*, London, 1957.
Dunbar, J.T., *History of Highland Dress*, London, 1962.
Giles, E.B., *The Art of Cutting and History of English Costume*, London, 1896.
Lawson, C.C.P., *A History of the Uniforms of the British Army*, London, five volumes, 1940-1967.
Mollo, J., *Military Fashion*, London, 1972.
Tylden, G., 'The Accoutrements of the British Infantryman, 1640 to 1940', JSAHR/57, London, 1979.
Waugh, N., *The Cut of Men's Clothes 1600-1900*, London, 1964.

17th to 18th centuries:

Barthorp, M., 'British Light Infantry Caps 1770-1799', MI/29, London, 1990.
Brzezinski, R., 'The Wings of the Polish Hussars: their origin and purpose', MI/88, London, 1995.
Carswell, A., 'Lt.Col. John Dalgleish, 21st Regiment of Foot, 1797', MI/16, London, 1989.
Chartrand, R., *Napoleonic Wars: Napoleon's Army*, BHU, London, 1996.
Childs, J., *Armies and Warfare in Europe*, Manchester, 1982.
Dempsey, G.C., *Napoleon's Soldiers*, London, 1994.
Edwards, E.H., 'Making the Redcoat: British Army Uniform Manufacture', MI/81, London, 1995.
Elliot-Wright, P.J.C., *English Civil War*, BHU, London, 1997.
Elting, J.R., *Napoleonic Uniforms*, two volumes, 1993.

Fletcher, I., *Napoleonic Wars: Wellington's Army*, BHU, London, 1996.
Haythornthwaite, P.J., 'The First Highland Regiment', MI/10, London, 1988.
Haythornthwaite, P., *The Austrian Army 1740-80*, OMAA, three volumes, London, 1994-95.
Lyndon, B., 'Military Dress and Uniformity 1680-1720', JSAHR/54, London, 1976.
Parker, G., *The Military Revolution*, Cambridge, 1996.
Reid, S., *King George's Army 1740-1793*, OMAA, London, three volumes, 1995-96.
Strachan, H., *British Military Uniforms 1768-1796*, London, 1975.
Tincey, J., *The British Army 1660-1704*, OMAA, London, 1994.
Zlatich, M., *General Washington's Army 1779-1783*, OMAA, two volumes, London, 1994-95.

19th century:

Barthorp, M., 'Infantry Undress Uniform 1822-1902', JSAHR/56, London, 1978.
Dervis, P.A., "The Old Red Coat': British Army Uniform Variations, India, 1880s-1920s', MI/16, London, 1989.
Farmer, J.S., *The Regimental Records of the British Army*, London, 1901.
Field, R., *American Civil War: Confederate Army*, BHU, London, 1996.
Field, R., *Mexican-American War 1846-48*, BHU, London, 1997.
Fosten, D.S.V., and Fosten, B.K., *The Thin Red Line*, London, 1987.
Guy, A.J., and Boyden, P.B., (editors), *Soldiers of the Raj*, London, 1997.
Harding, M. (editor), *The Victorian Soldier*, London, 1993.
Knight, I., *Go to your God like a soldier*, London, 1996.
Molloy, B., 'A Brief History of the Pickelhaube', MI/45, London, 1995.
Moore, A.J., 'The Regimental Jacket of Colour Sergeant William Nicholl 1822-25', MI/34, London, 1991.
Smith, R., *American Civil War: Union Army*, BHU, London, 1996.
Steppler, G.A., 'Redcoat: The Regimental Coat of the British Infantryman, c.1805-15', MI/20 & MI/22, two parts, London, 1989.
Strachan, H.F.A., 'The Origins of the 1855 Uniform Changes, An Example of Pre-Crimean Reform', JSAHR/55, London, 1977.

20th century:

Brayley, M.J., 'America's Women Soldiers: US Army Auxiliary Uniforms', MI/101 and MI/105, two parts, London, 1996.
Brayley, M.J., 'Blitzkrieg Warrior: German Army Uniform in Detail', MI/103 and MI/104, two parts, London, 1996.
Brayley, M., and Ingram, R., *World War II British Women's Uniforms*, Europa Militaria Special No.7, London, 1995.
Bull, S., 'Birth of a Classic: Developing the German Steel Helmet', MI/107, London, 1997.
Davis, B.L., *German Army Uniforms and Insignia 1933-1945*, London, 1971.
Hall, J.A., 'Silent Witness: German Infantry Tunic of a 1914 Casualty', MI/40, London, 1991.
Krawczyk, W., *German Army Uniforms of World War II*, London, 1995.
Lyles, K., *Vietnam: U.S. Uniforms*, Europa Militaria Special No.3, London, 1992.
Mahoney, K., 'US M1943 Field Jacket and Trousers', MI/49, London, 1992.
Mollo, A., *Uniforms of the SS*, London, 1997.
Newark, T., Newark, Q., and Borsarello, J.F., *Brassey's Book of Camouflage*, London, 1996.
Norris, J., 'Combat Soldier 1995: New British Army Combat Uniform', MI/70, London, 1994.
Norris, J., 'Modern Combat Helmets', MI/82, London, 1995.
Norris, J., 'Future Warrior, AD 2025', MI/86, London, 1995.

Rosignoli, G., *MVSN 1923-1943 Badges and Uniforms of the Italian Fascist Militia*, Farnham, 1980.
Shalito, A., Sauchenkov, I., and Mollo, A., *Red Army Uniforms of World War II*, London, 1993.
Shukman, D., *The Sorcerer's Challenge*, London, 1995.
Sylvia, S.W., and O'Donnell, M.J., *Uniforms, Weapons, and Equipment of the World War II G.I.*, Orange, Virginia, 1982.

DIRECTORY

Uniform collections:

National Army Museum, Royal Hospital Road, Chelsea, London SW3 4HT. Tells the history of the British Army.

Imperial War Museum, Lambeth Road, London. Warfare in the 20th century.

Guards Museum, Wellington Barracks, Birdcage Walk, London SW1A 2AX. Museum of the elite British regiments.

Smithsonian Institute, 14th & Constitution Avenue NW, Washington, D.C. 20560. The best collection of U.S. uniforms from the 18th century onwards, many gathered directly from army quartermaster supplies.

Musée de L'Armée, Hotel National des Invalides, Paris. The leading Napoleonic collection.

Musée Royale de L'Armée, Brussels. Remarkable array of 19th and 20th century uniforms.

Heeresgeschichtliches Museum, Vienna. Good on the early history of uniforms.

Uniform Manufacturers:

Andrew Clark (Military Metalwork) and Dawa Wood (Ages of Elegance), 1 Almond Grove, Brentford, Middlesex TW8 8NP (tel 0181 568 3210). Leading recreators of historic uniforms for British re-enactors.

Louis Chalmers, The Plumery, 16 Deans Close, Whitehall Gardens, Chiswick, London (tel: 0181 995 7099). Leading manufacturer of plumes and other headgear to the British Army and armies around the world. Also recreates historic hats, including Napoleonic shakos, for re-enactors.

C & D Jarnagin Company, PO Box 1860, Corinth, MS 38834 (tel: 601 2871977). Oldest established maker of Civil War uniforms for re-enactors in the U.S.

Hobson & Sons Ltd., Kenneth Road, Thundersley, Essex SS7 3AF (tel: 01268 793097). Leading British makers of uniforms and military equipment for the British Army and armies around the world.

Toye, Kenning & Spencer, Regalia House, Newtown Road, Bedworth, Warwickshire CV12 8QR (tel: 01203 315634). Badges and accoutrements.

Firmin & Sons PLC, 295 Regent Street, London W1R 7YA (tel: 0121 359 6666). Ceremonial dress and accoutrements.

Strines Textiles, Station Road, Strines, Nr Stockport, Cheshire SK12 3AQ (tel: 01663 764111). Printers of camouflage.

Abimelech Hainsworth, Spring Valley Mills, Stanningley, Pudsey, West Yorkshire LS28 6DW (tel: 0113 256 7407). Wool cloth and specialist textile merchants.

W.L. Gore and Associates (UK) Ltd., Simpson Parkway, Kirkton Campus, Livingstone, West Lothian, Scotland EH54 7BH (tel: 01506 412525). Makers of Gore-Tex.

Angels and Bermans, 40 Camden Street, London NW1 0EN (tel: 0171 836 5678). World's biggest entertainment costumiers, also hires out clothes and uniforms for fancy-dress parties.

Uniform dealers and retailers:

Regimentals, 70 Essex Road, Islington, London N1 8LT (tel: 0171 359 8579). Leading seller of uniforms and militaria from the 19th and 20th centuries.

The Old Brigade, 10a Harborough Road, Kingsthorpe, Northampton NN2 7AZ (tel: 01604 719389). WW2, mainly German militaria.

Adrian Forman, PO Box 25, Minehead, Somerset TA24 8YX (tel: 01643 862511). WW2, mainly German militaria.

Blunderbuss Antiques, 29 Thayer Street, London W1M 5LJ (tel: 0171 486 2444). WW1 and WW2 militaria.

Alan Beadle Antique Arms & Militaria, PO Box 1658, Dorchester, Dorset DT2 9YD (tel: 01308 897904). All periods, 1580-1945.

Mons Military Antiques, 221 Rainham Road, Rainham, Essex RM13 7SD (tel: 01277 810558). WW1 and WW2 militaria.

Silverman's, 2 Hartford Street, London E1 (tel: 0171 790 0900). Camouflage and contemporary military clothing.

Les Hussards de France, 4141 Pamona Avenue, Coconut Grove, Florida 33133, USA (tel: 305 665 5411). Napoleonic militaria.

The Bunker, 1842 E. 17th, PO Box 14196W2, Tulsa, OK 74159 1196, USA. WW1 and WW2 militaria.

Dale C. Anderson Co., 4 W.Confederate Avenue, Dept:A, Gettysburg, PA 17325, USA. Mail order catalogue, militaria 1776-1945.

J.C. Devine Inc, PO Box 413, 20 South St., Milford, NH 03055, USA (tel: 603 673 4967). Militaria auctioneers.

Black Cross Military Collectibles, PO Box 29767, Dept.C, Richmond, VA 23242, USA (tel: 804 740 4226). WW1 and WW2 militaria.

INDEX